THE PRINCIPAL AS

Data-Driven Leader

Introduction to the *Leading Student Achievement* Series

The *Leading Student Achievement* series is a joint publication of the Ontario Principals' Council (OPC) and Corwin Press as part of an active commitment to support and develop excellent school leadership. One of the roles of the OPC is to identify, design, develop, and deliver workshops that meet the learning needs of school leaders. Most of the handbooks in this series were originally developed as one-day workshops by their authors to share their expertise in key areas of school leadership. Following are the five handbooks in this series:

The Principal as Professional Learning Community Leader

The Principal as Data-Driven Leader

The Principal as Early Literacy Leader

The Principal as Instructional Leader in Literacy

The Principal as Mathematics Leader

Each handbook in the *Leading Student Achievement* series is grounded in action and is designed as a hands-on, practical guide to support school leaders in their roles as instructional leaders. From novice principals who are just assuming the principalship to experienced principals who are committed to continuous learning, readers from all levels of experience will benefit from the accessible blend of theory and practice presented in these handbooks. The practical strategies that principals can use immediately in their schools make this series a valuable resource to all who are committed to improving student achievement.

THE PRINCIPAL AS

Data-Driven Leader

LEADING STUDENT ACHIEVEMENT
SERIES

A Joint Publication

For information:

Corwin Press
A SAGE Company
2455 Teller Road
Thousand Oaks, California 91320
www.corwinpress.com

SAGE Ltd.
1 Oliver's Yard
55 City Road
London EC1Y 1SP
United Kingdom

SAGE India Pvt. Ltd.
B 1/I 1 Mohan Cooperative
Industrial Area
Mathura Road, New Delhi 110 044
India

SAGE Asia-Pacific Pte. Ltd.
33 Pekin Street #02-01
Far East Square
Singapore 048763

Printed in the United States of America

Library of Congress Cataloging-in-Publication Data

The principal as data-driven leader/Ontario Principals' Council.
    p. cm.
"A joint publication with Ontario Principals' Council."
Includes bibliographical references.
ISBN 978-1-4129-6304-6 (cloth)
ISBN 978-1-4129-6305-3 (pbk.)

    1. School improvement programs—Planning. 2. School improvement programs—Data processing. 3. School principals. 4. Educational leadership. I. Ontario Principals' Council. II. Title.

LB2822.8.P75 2009
371.2'07—dc22   2008035246

This book is printed on acid-free paper.

08   09   10   11   12   10 9 8 7 6 5 4 3 2 1

Acquisitions Editor:	Debra Stollenwerk
Editorial Assistant:	Allison Scott
Developmental Editor:	Daniel J. Richcreek
Production Editor:	Libby Larson
Copy Editor:	Paula L. Fleming
Typesetter:	C&M Digitals (P) Ltd.
Proofreader:	Theresa Kay
Indexer:	Maria Sosnowski
Cover Designer:	Lisa Riley

Contents

Acknowledgments

The Ontario Principals' Council gratefully acknowledges Rick Clark, the author of *The Principal as Data-Driven Leader*.

Rick Clark is currently an elementary school principal with the Hamilton-Wentworth District School Board in Ontario, Canada, a position he has held for over 20 years. Rick received his BA from McMaster University and his Masters of Education in Curriculum Studies from Brock University. He has taught educational research to Master of Education candidates at Daemen College in Buffalo, New York. During his career, Rick has also been president of the Ontario Middle Level Education Association, a case leader for the Ontario Teacher Qualifying Test, and a mentor for new principals. His interest in data-driven leadership began when he worked for the Educational Accountability and Quality Office in Ontario as a marker, group leader, and subject leader in mathematics. Rick and his wife, Kathy, have presented several workshops on the topic of data-driven school improvement planning both nationally and internationally and have worked as coaches with school staffs and departments as they plan, implement, and assess such plans.

The Ontario Principals' Council also wishes to acknowledge the contributions of the designers of the *Vital Signs* series of workshops about data-driven school management: Victor Chiasson, Kathy Clark, Marjorie Clegg, Gary Crocker, Terry Kennedy, Valerie Miyata, Ian Simpson, Sharon Speir, Pat Stanley, and Leona Woods. As well, the efforts of Ethne Cullen and Linda Massey in coordinating this joint OPC/Corwin project are gratefully acknowledged.

Corwin Press gratefully acknowledges the contributions of the following reviewers:

Kimberly Bright
Associate Professor of Educational Leadership
    and Special Education
Shippensburg University
Shippensburg, PA

Terry Crawley
Coordinator for School Planning and Professional
    Development
Archdiocese of Louisville
Louisville, KY

Dolores M. Gribouski
Principal
Columbus Park School
Worcester, MA

Mary Johnstone
Principal
Rabbit Creek Elementary School
Anchorage, AK

Dr. Richard Jones
Principal
Rochester Public School
Rochester, MN

Steve Knobl
Principal
Bayonet Point Middle School
New Port Richey, FL

Dr. Lawrence Kohn
Principal
Atascocita High School
Humble, TX

Introduction

The worldwide drive for accountability has created an environment in which schools in all developed countries are expected to show improvement in student achievement through the use of data, often based on the results of state or national assessments. But such information shows only the outcome of an instructional process, which may be informed by hunch or by fashion rather than grounded in real solutions to demonstrated, specific issues. This is where comprehensive, valid, reliable data (also referred to throughout this book as *evidence* or *information*) can be used to inform decision making and to improve student performance efficiently.

As school leaders, we have to make a choice in response to test scores: use the information available to work with staff through a data-driven school improvement process or just to change strategies based on what we already believe are the issues and hope that student performance improves. This book is designed to help school leaders who wish to make the former choice and work collaboratively with their staffs or departments, using evidence to "drill down" to discover the root causes of issues in student performance and to remedy them in an ongoing, accountable fashion. In particular, new administrators who do not have any experience in using data to inform curricular decisions will find this book helpful. Experienced administrators will find this book a concise summary and overview of the research in the area. It may also provide the experienced principal, assistant/vice principal, and department/grade head with some new tools and strategies to help refresh data-driven school improvement in their areas.

ORGANIZATION

Chapter 1 looks at the global drive for educational accountability and how that has led data-based school improvement planning as the most efficient and reliable method of both increasing student performance and improving the transparency of the process of continual school improvement.

Chapter 2 deals with the roles the principal plays in data-driven school improvement: leader, professional developer, and communicator. These are three essential roles successful principals must play during the improvement process, working within and without the school as model, mentor, monitor, mediator, and conduit for information. The principal is pivotal in the process, and the chapter explains how the principal can ensure that the improvement planning is successfully initiated, supported, and continued.

Chapter 3 outlines how a principal can successfully introduce data-driven school improvement planning, from convincing staff that such an endeavor has a great payoff to creating a culture of using broadly based data to inform all decisions.

Chapter 4 is about what data is and is not. The four types of data are defined, and activities are provided to help staff members understand the importance of gathering relevant, valid, complete, and reliable evidence of as many types as possible to ensure that decisions are based on the whole picture, not just part of it.

Chapter 5 describes the data-based school improvement planning cycle and how to use it to make, implement, and follow up on instructional plans based on good data.

Chapter 6 looks at refining the process once it is in place: using the concept of *root cause* to define issues further that need to be addressed and using the data-driven school improvement cycle to build SMART goals.

"Educator Toolkit": At the back of the book is an extensive toolkit of information to help the principal lead a school through the introduction and use of the data-driven school improvement planning cycle, as well as a glossary of commonly used terms and a list of suggested additional readings for those who wish to delve deeper.

This book will get you started on using data to inform, shape, revise, and assess your school improvement plan. It will start your school on a journey to true accountability and to demonstrable improvement in student performance.

CHAPTER 1

School Improvement Planning

S ocieties in the developed world at the beginning of the 21st century are complex and make many demands of their citizens. In the last 100 years, we have moved from an agricultural society, where 95 percent of the population worked and lived on farms; through an industrial age where the majority of work centered on heavy production; to an urban, technological society, where 95 percent of the population lives in urban or suburban centers and where most work is in service-oriented jobs. These wrenching changes in society necessitate great and continuing changes in the way we educate productive citizens, and the best way a principal and his or her school can keep up with these changes is through data-driven decision making.

While the relative isolation and economic independence of the farm has been replaced by the interdependence of urban living, the same process has been going on internationally: the economic independence of individual countries has been replaced by a web of global economic interdependence. Relatively highly paid workforces in the developed world cannot now compete with the lower labor costs of developing countries for manual labor jobs; those in the developed world must be ever more skilled to maintain a competitive edge. Employment, especially in the developed world, requires higher level thinking skills: Even the most menial job requires some sophistication in reading and in many aspects of mathematics. In a school setting, this means that principals and their staffs must constantly collect and use data to ensure that students are developing needed skills.

The Conference Board of Canada's Employability Skills Forum together with the Business and Education Forum on Science, Technology, and Mathematics gathered input from over 50 members representing business, government, and education and released, in May 2000, *Employability Skills 2000+*, "the critical skills you need in the workplace—whether you are self-employed or working for others" ("Apply Your Employability Skills at Work"). This document takes the increasingly complex skill set demanded by employers and breaks it into three parts:

Fundamental Skills

- Communicate
- Manage information
- Use numbers
- Think and solve problems

Personal Management Skills

- Demonstrate positive attitudes and behaviors
- Be responsible
- Be adaptable
- Learn continuously
- Work safely

Teamwork Skills

- Work with others
- Participate in projects and tasks

Similarly, the Partnership for 21st Century Skills, a consortium of 31 high-profile American companies, issued a *Framework for 21st Century Learning* in 2007. The Partnership begins by stating that, although mastery of core subjects (defined as including English, reading or language arts, world languages, arts, mathematics, economics, science, geography, history, and government and civics) is essential for students, the following 21st-century interdisciplinary themes must be interwoven within those core subjects:

- Global awareness
- Financial, economic, business, and entrepreneurial literacy
- Civic literacy
- Health literacy

The Partnership goes on to list the learning and innovation skills it believes will characterize students who are prepared for increasingly complex life and work environments in the future. Those skills include the following:

- Creativity and innovation
- Thinking skills and problem solving
- Communication and collaboration

It also lists the information, media, and technology skills students and citizens will need to be effective, including these:

- Information literacy
- Media literacy
- Information, communications, and technology (ICT) literacy

Finally, it maintains that living and working today and in the future will require more than just core knowledge and thinking skills. It states that to be successful, students will need to develop adequate life and career skills, such as the following:

- Flexibility and adaptability
- Initiative and self-direction
- Social and cross-cultural skills
- Productivity and accountability
- Leadership and responsibility

The world is changing, and the skills required for students to be successful in the world of their future are also changing. Education systems across the developed world, part of whose mandate is to prepare students to become productive citizens, have thus had to shift from a curriculum focused on "three Rs" to one designed to build student competency in the above skills. Instead of "Reading," which was defined as comprehending print, and "'Riting," defined as being able to express oneself using pen, pencil, and paper, schools are now charged with teaching students to communicate effectively in many forms, including reading print and nonprint media and critically evaluating books, periodicals, material from the media and the Internet, and so on, as well as being able to express themselves clearly and cogently in a wide variety of media. Instead of "'Rithmetic," the manipulation of numbers, schools must now teach numeracy, the understanding of numbers and how to solve mathematical problems. In addition, management skills and teamwork skills that were not taught in the past have now become expectations. At the same time, schools and school systems are more accountable than ever before.

THE INTERNATIONAL DRIVE FOR ACCOUNTABILITY IN EDUCATION

In the last two decades, a tidal wave of accountability has swept around the world. Increasingly, organizations, whether in the private or public sectors, have been measured by the quality as well as the quantity of their products or services. At the same time, there has been a huge trend toward teamwork and cooperation in all aspects of life. Not surprisingly, schools have not been immune to these trends: All around the developed world, taxpayers are demanding proof that the tax dollars they are spending on the public school system (or the money they are spending to send their children to private schools) are resulting in educated students who can read, write, solve mathematical problems, and have some fluency in second (or third) languages and the arts. That proof, whether to inform a school community, a state or national agency, or international comparative studies, can only come in the form of data provided by schools. The gathering of such information on a national scale is epitomized by the No Child Left Behind legislation in the United States and in the Every Child Matters apparatus in the United Kingdom. At the same time, stakeholders want a say in how schools are run to ensure that the data show that students are achieving these goals.

Politicians across the developed world have responded to changes in societal needs: The desire for accountability in all public institutions and the need for teaming and economic pressures to legislate change are at an unprecedented level. Wherever educators look, in the United States, in the United Kingdom, in Australia, in Canada, in the European Union, in Singapore, and elsewhere, legislation has mandated new educational targets backed by large-scale assessment and data collection with attendant rewards and penalties.

The Pillars of Government Education Policy

Governments expect changes in education to be tracked. Educators know that appropriate, complete data is the only way to inform school decision making correctly on the way to meet defined targets. With appropriate evidence informing school decisions, educators are expected to progress in five major strands toward excellence (see Figure 1.1 on page 8), explained more fully below. Each strand, required to be demonstrated through the use of school-based evidence, is felt to be essential to excellence in education and is defined by student success.

Public Accountability

Societies value their schools and recognize that the educational level of the population within a country is a strong indicator of the economic health of that country. For that reason, governments and the people they represent are willing to finance public education. But they want to ensure that their money is being spent effectively and that children are being educated properly. They require evidence of an adequate return on their investment— that the money spent is demonstrably benefiting the state at the best possible rate.

Student Achievement

The focus of education is student achievement. In the words of Brian Benzel, superintendent, Spokane (Washington) Public Schools, "We wanted to make sure that a year's worth of instruction was resulting in a year's worth of gains" (AASA, 2002, p. 10). Governments and the people they represent want a good rate of return on their investments, and the true measure of the output of the education system is change in student achievement

Figure 1.1   Pillars of Government Education Policy

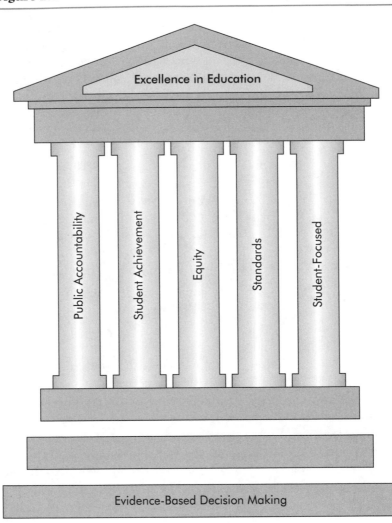

over time. This can only be measured through the use of assessment data, where student achievement is compared to a standard and those assessments are evaluated and reported.

Equity

In the past 30 or so years, the public has demanded that education be inclusive: that no child is left behind. Today's schools welcome every child and must provide education for all students with special needs, as each child is expected to learn to the best of his or her ability. Similarly, increased immigration has resulted in an increase of students whose first language is not English, and schools are expected to provide appropriate educational opportunities while assisting these students to acquire mastery in English. Schools are required to demonstrate that this is happening and that any extra funding is being used to provide equity of opportunity for all students.

Standards

As society has become more multinational, people have become more aware of the need to compete internationally. Industries have to compete in a global environment, and they then require that their workforce be equivalent or superior in knowledge and skill level to others across the world. This, in essence, means that to be globally competitive, states need a workforce that is educated by a public education system that matches that of any other state. Thus, curricula across the world have become more uniform, and state-to-state as well as country-to-country comparisons, through national and international testing, have become commonplace.

Schools are being measured for return on investment, and only valid data based on international standards can provide authentic comparisons.

Student Focused

Today governments all across the developed world are calling for public accountability, equity, and a focus on student achievement as measured against international standards as pillars of educational policy. They are requiring evidence to demonstrate that these public policy goals are being met, that the pillars are standing and fully formed, and that the result will inevitably be excellence in public education.

School administrators now need to deal with the new demands caused by such increased accountability and the growing need to work cooperatively with the school community of staff, parents, community leaders, and, in middle and secondary schools, students. Principals need an open process to collect relevant local information and to work with teams to use that evidence to create movement toward stated school goals, especially student success. They also need a factual base from which to demonstrate such movement and student success to continue to form a basis for positive, productive partnerships within and without the school community.

Both needs can be built only from the appropriate use of data or evidence.

Improving Student Achievement

Victoria L. Bernhardt (1998) gives the example of a high school in rural northern California, where 95 percent of graduates did not complete their first year of college (p. 10). Assuming that the graduates lacked the appropriate social skills for success in a university setting, the school district concentrated efforts on remedying this lack. However, the lack of success continued. Not until interviews were done with returning students did the district find that the real cause of the problem was the students' inability to write at the university level. When this issue was addressed, most graduates became successful in college, and the district began to use data to inform decisions.

Similarly, an elementary school in a rapidly growing area in Ontario, Canada, found that few students were enrolling in their kindergarten programs that were offered on a half-day basis. Parents often delayed enrollment until the first grade, when attendance is mandatory. That often presented a curricular challenge to the school. Research into parental demographics quickly disclosed that in most families, both parents worked full-time and that often those parents had fairly long commutes to get to their place of employment. Further inquiry revealed that these families often needed day care all day every day and the half-day program did not meet their needs. When the school began to offer a licensed day care facility that accepted children early in the morning, fed into the kindergarten program, and minded the children for the other half of the day and after school, enrollment soared.

As Lorna Earl and Steven Katz (2006) write:

> When policy makers and school personnel either ignore data or rely on inadequate data, they run the risk of making poor decisions. Without good data, school personnel may be blindsided

or make decisions based upon individual perceptions, opinions, and limited observations. Valuable time, energy, and resources are wasted when new programs and practices are adopted that apply foreign organizational cultures, lack evidence of effectiveness, or do not match up with student needs. The effect on students and their learning is even more important than the loss of time and energy, as another month or year passes without the implementation of effective strategies. (p. 6)

But having the complete, relevant data is still not enough. Data must ultimately be used to improve student performance. Schools must be focused, through a plan, on increasing student success, and that plan cannot only be based on whether or not the students reached the standards in the required time; it must be incremental and measure progress toward those goals. International testing is not enough. To be accountable, to improve student achievement equitably toward reaching or surpassing international standards, all resources in the educational system, be they human or financial, must be directed to improving student achievement. There must be a plan for how to get students to the point where they can compete successfully internationally, and that plan must be verified by evidence.

SCHOOL IMPROVEMENT PLANNING FOR STUDENT ACHIEVEMENT

Every school, school district, state, and country wants its students to be successful. To do so, each must clearly define what that success will look like (create a target) so that it knows what it is aiming for. Schools can only change successfully when they focus on specific goals, develop strategies to reach those goals, and monitor their progress with feedback loops. School improvement planning is a process for doing just that: setting goals for improvement in student performance, making decisions about how to achieve those goals, and creating monitoring systems to ensure that the school is moving toward those goals. The ultimate objective is always to improve student achievement in the areas designated by the country, state, district, and school in ways relevant to the individual school in context.

School improvement planning is so important that it has been mandated across the developed world.

School improvement plans are selective: they help principals, teachers and [parents] answer the questions "What will we focus on now?' and "What will we leave until later?" They encourage staff and parents to monitor student achievement levels and other factors, such as school environment, that are known to influence student success. With up-to-date information about how well students are performing, schools are better able to respond to the needs of students, teachers and parents.

A school plan is also a mechanism through which the public can hold schools accountable for student success and through which it can measure improvement. (Education Improvement Commission, Ontario Ministry of Education, 2000)

School improvement is the single most important business of the school, in that it is the process schools use to ensure that all students are achieving at high levels. The continuous School Improvement Planning Cycle is the process used to coordinate and prioritize all the work of the school in the context of student achievement. (State of Washington, Superintendent of Public Instruction, 2006)

Keeping School Planning on Track

Effective school planning works much like a space probe. Using all the evidence available, a target is chosen, and the rocket is fired. Immediately, positional data are sent back to the control center by the missile. Controllers then compare those data with the information they have about where the missile should be going given the planned trajectory. If everything is going as planned, the controllers do nothing, but if there is a difference between where the rocket is supposed to be and where it is, they can make corrections by firing steering rockets to get the probe back on course. This exchange of information and corrective action happens almost continuously so that large corrections are unnecessary and the probe will reach its target. Without continuous course corrections, the probe would most likely stray off track and never reach its goal. Similarly, school planning can easily get off track and never have its intended outcomes.

As an example, the state test scores of a school showed that its students were weak in problem-solving skills in mathematics. The school invested much time and money over the next year in designing a plan and working with its students to improve mathematical problem-solving skills. Much emphasis was placed on translating word problems into mathematical statements, then working through the mathematics and stating the answer. Staff and parents alike awaited the results of the next year's testing. Alas, the score in mathematical problem solving had not improved at all. Disappointed and somewhat angry, The staff at first blamed the testing organization but then began looking at individual test papers to find out what was causing the continued poor scores. To their surprise, they soon found the issue: the test asked students to describe how they had solved the problem, and their students had not been able to describe their process effectively in writing. The next year, the school emphasized verbalization of the process of solution and checked that students could do this by using mock testing. Scores improved dramatically on the next state test.

Sorting Through the Available Data

Data, especially the kind generated by No Child Left Behind and Every Child Matters, are now available to almost every school in the developed world. However, the question still remains as to whether or not they are being used effectively for school improvement planning.

As Alan Greenblatt (2007) writes,

No Child Left Behind will continue to move states and districts in two different directions. On the one hand, there will be some that try to fudge the numbers as best they can in order to make themselves look better. They will, in effect, be lying to students and parents about whether kids are actually proficient in basic subjects.

On the other hand, an increasing number of states and districts will be using data more confidently and aggressively in order to aid instruction. For them, the data requirements of No Child Left Behind have whetted an appetite for more and better data that does not merely show standardized results but can inform improvements in the classroom. ("Two Different Directions")

In other words, many schools and districts are actively seeking rich data to inform and make decisions about their school improvement planning. Such information is crucial to the validity of the school planning process; without it, schools wander in the wilderness without reliable signposts or landmarks. The landscape is all shifting sand, and progress toward the goal is erratic and improbable.

Sometimes decision making around the school improvement plan has been based on intuition, tradition, or convenience. This results in the following:

- Scattered staff development programs
- Budgetary decisions based on prior practice or priority programs
- Staff assignments based on interest and availability
- Reports to the community about school events
- Goal setting by board members, administrators, or teachers, based on votes, favorite initiatives, or fads
- Staff meetings that focus on operations and the dissemination of information
- Parent communication via twice-a-year conferences, open houses, and newsletters
- Grading systems based on each teacher's criteria of completed work and participation
- Periodic administrative team meetings focused solely on operations

However, when decision making is based on data, the following can result:

- Focused staff development programs as an improvement strategy to address problems/needs identified by the data
- Budget allocations to programs based on data-informed needs
- Staff assignments based on skills needed as indicated by the data
- Organized, factual reports to the community about the learning progress of students

- Goal setting based on data about problems and possible explanations
- Staff meetings that focus on strategies and issues raised by the local school's data
- Regular parent communication regarding the progress of their children informed by specific data
- Grading systems based on common criteria for student performance that report progress toward the standards as well as work skills
- Administrative team meetings that focus on measured progress toward data-based improvement goals (Technology Alliance, 2005)

Without valid, reliable, complete, and consistent information, the school improvement plan will rarely result in true improvement. If the evidence is not valid, the inferences and conclusions drawn from it are unlikely to be either useful or accurate—the evidence must actually measure what it is intending to measure, and the sample must be large enough not to be influenced by sampling error. If there are questions about the reliability of the information, those questions apply to any conclusions or inferences drawn from that information. Reliability can be certain when information is consistent with other information. Only then we can be sure that data were collected in a trustworthy manner and that the instruments used to collect them were well designed and implemented. If data are inconsistent, they are probably either invalid or unreliable or both and should not be used. When evidence about the same thing drawn from the same students is consistent (not necessarily exactly the same), it is probably reliable and valid. The quality of the evidence collected certainly has a direct impact on the quality of the conclusions reached and, thus, the quality of the school improvement plan. The scope of the evidence collected has a similar impact.

There has been much discussion about *what* information to use in making informed instructional decisions. Large-scale assessment, such as that mandated by No Child Left Behind and Every Child Matters, is often the only data used, yet it is only part of the picture—a slice of information about how students perform on certain forms of testing at certain points of their educational careers. The data often arrive well after the time of testing, further complicating matters. Throughout this book, we will emphasize the use of other information, such as demographic data, classroom assessments, and analyses of how instruction takes place in the classrooms, to flesh out the standardized assessment information collected throughout the developed world.

SUMMARY

Many major shifts in culture have happened and continue to happen across the world, including the globalization of the economy, the changing nature of workplace needs, and the rising demand for accountability. All of these have had an impact on education. As the skills, knowledge, and attributes of a successful graduate have changed, as noted by such prestigious institutions as the Partnership for 21st Century Skills, the education needed by that graduate has changed and with it, the demand on our schools to provide that education. Principals, as school leaders, have become accountable on a local, state, and national level to provide evidence that their schools are equipping students to be successful in the 21st century.

Governments around the world, as funders of public school systems, are building accountability systems, such as No Child Left Behind and Every Child Matters, to attempt to ensure that every school is meeting requirements of equity, student focus, and transparent accountability about student achievement with a goal of meeting mandated standards. Schools and districts with a real interest in fostering the success of their students embrace this accountability and take it further than collecting and using the required data; they collect a much wider evidential base and use it in every aspect of the modification and improvement of instructional processes.

As we know, measuring the end product cannot change the outcome unless there are changes in the process of instruction informed by the gaps between the received data and the intended outcomes. The school improvement planning cycle is the essential and critical mechanism that translates the analysis of the evidence into a plan to change instruction and improve the data in intended ways. It is the link joining collected information to changing what goes on in classrooms and in the school, and it relies on the collected information being valid, reliable, consistent, and comprehensive.

Throughout this book, we shall be looking at the use of widely based evidence in planning, implementing, and reviewing change in a school in two ways. The first is educational: What are "good" data, where and how can they be gathered, and in what ways can they be used most effectively? The second looks at the principal's role: How does an administrator teach staff, students, and community to use evidence well through all phases of the school improvement process? As we will explore in the next chapter, the principal is the key player in leading a school through a data-based school improvement cycle, and in this role, she or he has three critical dimensions.

C H A P T E R   2

The Dimensions of the Principal as Data-Driven Leader

In Chapter 1, we looked at the need for every school to build a school improvement planning cycle based on data that are valid, reliable, consistent, and comprehensive. As we will see in this chapter, the principal is the key to such a process. As the prime instructional leader in the school, the principal is the person who can effectively captain the implementation of improvement through planning or can frustrate such change. The principal's role is a pivotal one.

Just as your school teams need to collect data constantly to ensure that the implemented school plans are making the differences they were designed to make, so you as principal must constantly examine whether or not you are on the right path in leading the process of collecting and using evidence to create, implement, and assess a school improvement plan to improve student performance in your school.

The role of the principal may be broken down into three dimensions in leading the data-driven improvement process: leader, professional developer, and communicator.

THE PRINCIPAL AS LEADER

It is clear that the principal is the prime instructional leader in the school; such a role is often enshrined in legislation as well as in practice. To lead effectively, the principal must have a passion for school improvement, a clear vision of the process, a plan for implementation, and a process for aligning resources to support the process.

As leader, the principal sets the tone of her school. Every minute of every day, the principal must "walk the talk" by exhibiting a passion for the improvement of student performance. Whether it is in casual conversations with parents or staff members, in parent council meetings, in written communications, in interactions with superiors, or in the public forum, the principal must lead by exhibiting that enthusiasm and dedication. Eventually such a leader comes to embody that quest for the best possible ways of assisting each student to learn, and the school gets the same reputation.

This passion must be genuine and consistent to ensure a beneficial and organized approach. Consistency from the principal will become part of the school culture, as we will discuss in Chapter 3. The principal's actions must always align with what she claims to espouse, or that principal will end up sending double messages. A leader can't ask people to do what she says rather than what she does. The principal must show staff, students, and community that evidence must be used to make decisions, thus demonstrating both how data-driven decision making is done and how effective it is. The chart in Figure 2.1 will work as both a reminder of the aspects of being a leader and as a checklist of actions performed.

Understanding and Implementing the Process

Chapters 3 through 6 of this book explain a comprehensive process for using data to build, implement, and evaluate a school improvement plan to improve student success. The principal must understand this process as a whole before starting to plan implementation, for using bits and pieces will not only result in a poor plan but will also create frustration and disillusionment with the entire planning process.

To lead staff effectively through data collection, data analysis, the development of a school plan to improve instruction, and reviews of the effectiveness of the school plan, the principal must be able to explain the process to staff, parents, and the community. And to do this properly, he must have a data-based school

Figure 2.1 The Principal's Role as Leader

	What data show that I am doing this?
✓ Do I create a passion for school improvement?	
✓ Do I model evidence-based decision making?	
✓ Do I understand the process?	
✓ Do I have a plan for data-driven school improvement?	
✓ Do I have staff teams in place to lead and drive the process?	
✓ Are structures in place to facilitate teamwork?	
✓ Am I assessing the implementation of the plan?	
✓ Do I ensure that the school budget aligns with our goals?	
✓ Am I staffing to meet the plan?	
✓ Is the school being restructured to meet the needs of the plan?	

© Queen's Printer for Ontario, 2000. Reprinted with permission.

improvement planning implementation plan based on an effective model and specific to his school.

Aligning Great Teams

A principal trying to change a school alone is like a single person trying to push a freight train—nearly impossible. But if teams of staff members, parents, and students are all pushing in the same direction, the train will start to move. The power of many teams is the engine of school improvement; without those people in place, lasting change is unlikely. When teachers power the improvement plan, changes happen not only in the school but in the classroom, where it really matters.

Steven Covey (2001), in his "Four Roles of Leadership for Educators" course, speaks of the "filters" that have to be in place to ensure organizational change. One of these is having the right structures. The facilitation of team meetings and opportunities for teams to communicate with each other and with the entire organization are essential. Without this, the momentum of the teams will falter, and any change will occur only in isolated pockets. As leader, the principal must provide time and opportunity for communication and rewards to school improvement teams to enable them to work effectively.

Assessing the Ongoing Progress

Frequent assessment must be made to keep your team on target; when it's not, changes must be made to ensure the program continues on the correct path. As instructional leader, the principal is responsible for ensuring that desired improvement is really happening. Use of evidence is not just diagnostic or summative; it is formative. By demonstrating the collection of formative as well as summative data, the principal sets examples for others, keeping their plans on target, too. Finally, others need to know if the plans are progressing in the right direction. Staff, students, parents, and community all need to be kept in the loop, and that can only be done through regular assessment of the process.

Ensuring that the school budget aligns with the plan is absolutely key and very simple to check. Every time a teacher, department head, student, or parent asks for money for a project, the principal's reply should be, "How does that align with our plans?" Principals know that they have met this expectation when a teacher comes into the office and states that funding for an activity is crucial because it matches specific, quoted goals and that data will be collected to indicate whether or not the activity did, indeed, advance the school toward those goals.

While it is very hard to deny worthy requests that do not match the goals, doing so is necessary, both to devote more resources to reaching those goals and to demonstrate that the school is indeed on a path and cannot be diverted by anything other than relevant data.

Assigning Staff to Support the School Plan

When staffing a school, allocation of personnel should reflect the implementation of the improvement plan. It is the role of the principal to ensure that this happens. For instance, if a key element of the improvement plan in an elementary school is the provision of support to struggling early readers, staffing must include extra literacy teachers in the primary grades, even if it means larger class sizes in other grades. Similarly, in a secondary school that is planning extra emphasis on meeting the needs of students for whom English is a second language, teachers must be allocated to do this task, even at some expense to other areas.

If the school improvement plan is, indeed, to be the blueprint for education at the school, the builders must follow the blueprint. The shape of the school day, the timetable, and supervision schedules—all should, within the context of policies and collective agreements, reflect the school improvement plan. For instance, if the plan states that grade or subject teams will meet to collect and analyze information and to discuss the implementation of new instructional practices on a weekly basis, the timetable must allow for such discussion. If the plan requires adult mentors for at-risk students, time must be created for the mentors to meet with those students. If such structures are not present, the plan will not be implemented. The principal must ensure that structures facilitate the implementation of the plan.

THE PRINCIPAL AS PROFESSIONAL DEVELOPER

In most schools, teachers and parents are unfamiliar with using data to drive, monitor, and assess an effective school improvement plan. It is up to the principal, directly or indirectly, to provide support in the form of professional development primarily to staff and the community. This will help ensure that teachers have the skills and knowledge to build, implement, and assess the plan and that parents understand what is happening at their children's school. Thus, the principal must ensure that support is available to help staff and the community understand the process; to gather appropriate, valid, reliable, comprehensive data; to analyze the information; and to support all phases of the school plan.

Teachers need to know where they are going as they embark on what will be a long process that may challenge them. Among other things, as an individual school, your data collection resources may be limited. It is up to the principal, as professional developer, to enable staff to learn about and access available sources of data. Some districts have "data warehouses," computerized storehouses of information with the capability of comparing one source of information with another. Some agencies, such as the U.S. Census, provide huge banks of information, and social planning agencies have a lot of available information—there are many sources of information available for anyone willing to dig it up.

It is also pointless and frustrating to reinvent the wheel. Often, groups of schools, districts, provinces, or states offer valid, reliable tools to collect evidence. As an example, when bullying became a hot topic, many schools began to try to collect information about the issue in their locations, using tools that were laboriously created and may not have had a lot of validity. In an initiative led by principals, one district in Canada partnered with the psychology department of a local university to create a valid, reliable tool that was simple to apply from Grades 1 to 12 and created a full picture of real and perceived bullying issues. The survey was administered at 55 participating schools, each of which got good evidence about that school and summary data from all participating schools. The chart in Figure 2.2 can be used as a checklist when approaching professional development as a principal.

Figure 2.2   The Principal's Role as Professional Developer

	What data show that I am doing this?
✓ Do I understand the process and help all involved share that understanding?	
✓ Do I assist all staff in understanding how to gather valid, reliable, consistent, comprehensive data?	
✓ Do I support all staff in learning how to analyze data?	
✓ Do I facilitate the professional development needed by staff members as they begin to select strategies?	
✓ Do I facilitate the professional development needed by staff members as they implement new strategies and structures?	

Analyzing the Data

As philosopher Fernando Flores is widely reported to have said, "An organization's results are determined through webs of human commitments, born in webs of human conversations" (Brown & Isaacs, 1996/1997, p. 2). One example of this type of analysis through conversation would be that at one school, report card marks in Grade 5 mathematics were significantly higher in one class than in the other two classes. The principal brought the teachers together and walked them through the data use cycle with the class averages and medians in mathematics. The teachers, through the comparison of their predictions with the evidence, began to talk about how they assessed, evaluated, and reported student achievement in mathematics. Eventually they came up with a plan to use common assessment tools and to mark the work of students from other classes so that each summative piece was marked by two teachers, who then compared assessments and discussed why they had given the grades they had assigned. Not only did the distribution of marks on reports become similar for each class, but the validity of the assessments increased greatly.

Supporting the School Plan

Professional development time in a school is often a scarce resource and must be used as wisely as possible. As the famous quote says, "The main thing is to keep the main thing the main thing." It is very easy to get distracted by the flavor of the month; by state, provincial, or district demands; or by parental requests. But once a school embarks on the school planning process, it is, indeed, the main thing and deserves all the professional development time available. Devoting all available professional development time to working on the school plan also demonstrates that the purpose of professional development is primarily to advance the plan and to increase student achievement.

Teachers have many skills, and often they can use their talents to assist in the process. For example, a teacher with postgraduate work in the teaching of reading can assist others in data collection and interpretation involving reading, a teacher with an interest in visuals can prepare graphic representations of data, and teachers with backgrounds in statistics can crunch data into manageable bits.

One principal who had links to a local university, with district support and approval, offered his staff opportunities to audit university-level courses during the school day, if they could show how such experiences would assist in the implementation of the school plan and if they could arrange coverage for their classes. Amazingly, over a third of the staff took him up on his offer and brought their enriched, current information back to their colleagues in the school community for use in planning, implementation, and review, thereby assisting the process as a whole.

In another school, teachers saw a need to go beyond differentiated instruction in providing appropriate learning opportunities for the large number of challenged students in their secondary school. The principal facilitated a team of staff who arranged for a credit course in special education to be offered to the whole staff in after-school sessions. A large majority of the staff, propelled by their commitment to the school plan, took the course to improve their instructional practices.

THE PRINCIPAL'S ROLE AS COMMUNICATOR

Principals must lead in communicating a shared vision that builds a commitment of staff, students, parents, and the community to the school improvement plan. They must also lead in informing all stakeholders of the planning process and in explaining how data are used to create, mold, and evaluate the plan. It has often been said that a school vision is not really a school vision until every member of the school community not only knows what the vision is but can communicate it. The principal's ability to communicate the vision of the school is directly linked to the use of data to build, implement, and assess a school plan that will demonstrably lead to the explicitly stated preferred future for students in the school.

Demographic data are essential to the understanding of the culture of any school. Small schools are different from large schools, urban schools from rural schools, schools with large non-English-speaking populations from those with mostly unilingual English-speaking students. Descriptions of the school population and school culture help the community understand the school's demographics and other parameters and form a basis for how that school will begin an improvement plan. The principal should be responsible for sharing this information with staff and with the community. A checklist for the principal's role as a communicator is presented in Figure 2.3.

Figure 2.3   The Principal's Role as Communicator

	What data show that I am doing this?
✓ Do I clearly communicate the vision of the school and of data-driven school improvement? ✓ Am I constantly informing stakeholders about the process and our progress? ✓ Have I ensured that all staff members can articulate the data they are using and how they are using it? ✓ Am I using evidence when I am communicating about the school?	

© Queen's Printer for Ontario, 2000. Reprinted with permission.

Informing Stakeholders About the Process

If travelers don't have an explicit road map, they get lost. In the same sense, all members of the school community need to know both where they are going (goals) and how they will get there (process). Not only must the principal explain the planning or data use process clearly, she must be seen to do so.

If a school is to improve student performance, all staff members must be able to articulate what evidence they in particular and the school in general are collecting to check that such performance is indeed improving. If each staff member can see her part clearly and see how her part fits into the jigsaw puzzle of the whole school, then she should be able to explain the data sources and their application to parents, students, and the community. Everyone can clearly demonstrate that they are on the same page and that the page leads to improved student performance.

Communicating How to Use Data in the Context of School Planning

The principal, as spokesperson for the school, is in a unique position to stress constantly how data are used in making all school decisions, especially those in the school planning process. Just as a principal would not suspend a student from school without data about that student's conduct, so changes to the school plan must be seen to be based on evidence.

For instance, one large rural high school in northern Canada had a reputation for violence, and many in the community believed that the school plan should primarily deal with that issue. The staff and students designed and completed an in-depth study about violence in the school and found that it was really not an issue—the violence was taking place outside the school. Armed with that evidence, the staff could factually inform parents about the difference between perception and reality and could approach community agencies to deal with the level of violence at places identified as "hot spots" within the community.

The school was "walking the talk": using evidence from a reliable, valid source to communicate about a school issue, setting the stage for basing the school plan on reliable, valid data.

SUMMARY

The principal must have a clear understanding of the entire process of data-driven school improvement and a plan developed for putting that process into action in the school, having taken into account the culture and demographics of that school. He must develop teams of staff members (and, sometimes, students and community members) who will drive the process so that the initiative will not only be powered from within but will really take root and be long lasting. The principal also ensures that the right structures within the school, such as opportunities to collect and analyze data, are in place.

The principal as leader must be able to take on the three roles discussed above (leader, professional developer, and communicator) to ensure the progress of a successful school improvement plan. She must be able to assess, correct, and model assessment constantly for learning and demonstrate her commitment to the successful implementation of the process. She should build a capacity for the collection and analysis of reliable, valid, consistent, and comprehensive data in staff members so that they can participate fully in the process and facilitate access to sources of information. And it is up to the principal to communicate both within and outside the school all aspects of that process.

With those dimensions clearly in mind, we can now begin the process. The next chapter will discuss how to convince staff that data-driven school improvement is worthwhile, and it will show how to embark on the first steps in the process.

CHAPTER 3

Introducing Data-Based School Improvement

The principal as leader, communicator, and professional developer can work with the full school community to develop a culture where the school improvement process can become entirely data driven and, thus, transparent and accountable. Getting this schoolwide culture of data-driven management in place will take time. Working through the suggested learnings and exercises in the following pages will occur at an individual pace at each school. Each new step will take time to digest and consolidate, each school will have different needs and resources, and each staff and community will begin from a slightly different place.

Because this process is truly a big change, it is important that it is introduced slowly. Staff must first realize that evidence-based school assessment and improvement planning is useful, international, pervasive, and research based. Teams will then learn to choose meaningful, valid information; process it appropriately; develop improvement plans based on their interpretation; and gather further evidence to examine whether the actions taken are causing the intended outcomes. Learning and internalizing this process will take some time. Rushing to get more immediate results will only result in superficial learnings, which will often result in misguided planning and little effective improvement.

If you, the principal, take your time to ensure that learnings are internalized through practice and focused conversation, the culture of the school will change, and staff, students, and parents will begin to base planning on demonstrated needs and measure achievement in a clear, transparent manner. In many schools, this has led to learning communities where groups of teachers have attempted "pilot" innovations in single classrooms, based on gap analysis created through data collection and research. The teacher or teachers doing the pilot continually check to be sure the innovation is bearing fruit—if not, it is jettisoned and the teachers move on; if it is moving toward the intended outcome, it can then be adopted by the whole group. The culture of the school then becomes one of innovation based on clear evidence and research.

The possibilities are endless, but every plan must start at the beginning.

CONVINCING SCHOOL STAFF

The first responsibility of a principal as leader in implementing the school improvement plan is to reinforce with staff, students, and the community the importance of evidence in measuring the success of the school at improving student achievement. School staffs are often dubious about new initiatives for many reasons. Some have seen many such ideas come and go and take the attitude that "this too shall pass." Others are very comfortable in their teaching style and truly believe that they are using the most effective instructional methods available. Others may be afraid of the unknown, and a few may be simply opposed to the concept of change. However, most teachers entered the profession out of a desire to help children and young adults learn and become successful; these teachers are ready to listen to anything that can help them in their quest.

The role of the principal at this point is to show each teacher that data-driven school improvement is in fact nothing new; that it is a clear, transparent process that can demonstrably increase student learning; that it can be done in most cases without abandoning good teaching practices (in fact, it will demonstrate what is indeed good practice and reinforce it); and that each teacher will have support in showing improvement. Finally, staff need to be aware that the use of data to assess instruction is not a passing fancy but instead is international and permanent and that only by embracing reliable, valid data about their own instruction in the context of their classrooms will they be able to demonstrate high student achievement and defend their own instructional practices.

Introducing the Concepts

One way to get staff members to begin to talk meaningfully about data-driven school improvement planning is through the use of relevant and stimulating quotations as a springboard for discussion. This should be done with the entire faculty present, such as at a staff meeting. You begin by taking some relevant news items, or some quotes about the use of evidence, and photocopying them onto large pieces of colored paper, preferably ledger-sized paper, using a different color for each news item or quote. Cut each piece of paper into at least three pieces. (See Resource A: Sample Quotes in the "Educator Toolkit" at the back of the book for a reproducible copy of these quotes.)

When members of the group begin to arrive, hand them a piece of the cut-up paper randomly. To begin the meeting, ask them to find those who have the rest of their "puzzle" (the colors will really help here), then discuss the quote or news item as a small group. After adequate discussion time (often ten minutes or so), they then briefly share their discussion with the whole group in an oral presentation. Not only does this exercise focus the participants on the use of evidence and student standards, it should reform the group, through the random distribution of puzzle pieces, and can break up "like" groups who usually sit together.

The next step is to make teachers aware of the global sweep of data-based accountability. It is easy to Google something like "student testing results news" and get millions of hits. Again, news articles like those in Figure 3.1 on pages 34 to 36 can be photocopied, again with groups discussing them and giving brief oral reports about their discussions. Through the range of articles, teachers will be presented with the scope and sweep of student testing, a form of data collection.

Ask staff members to focus on the question "Why is it important to use evidence in your school-based decision making?" and the questions you have in your school. In groups of four or eight,

Figure 3.1   News Articles on Data-Based Accountability in Education

---

Math + Test = Trouble for U.S. economy

First-of-its-kind study shows U.S. lags many other nations in real-life math skills

WASHINGTON—For a nation committed to preparing students for 21st-century jobs, the results of the first-of-its-kind study of how well teenagers can apply math skills to real-life problems is sobering.

Christian Science Monitor, December 7, 2004

Dryden Schools Address Reading Issues

DRYDEN, NY—Educators in the Dryden Central District know their state English test scores aren't up to par—or at least, what they could be. So, in the wake of Dryden students' most recent performance on state subject tests, school leaders are taking the bull by the horns when it comes to reading instruction.

The Ithaca Journal (Ithaca, NY), March 25, 2005

Bentley Primary Kids Out-Read Competitors Across the Country

WICHITA, KS—When kids at Bentley Primary School received a letter on Friday from First Lady Laura Bush congratulating them on winning a national reading contest, they cheered.

The Wichita Eagle (Wichita, KS), March 21, 2005

Performance-Based Contracts Planned for School Principals

SYDNEY—The Labor Government in the Australian state of New South Wales (NSW) has introduced measures allowing it to dismiss public school principals who fail to meet as yet unspecified performance criteria.

World Socialist Web Site, November 17, 2004

School Standard Rise "Overstated"

The official statistics watchdog has said rising primary school test scores in England "substantially" overstated the rise in education standards. The Statistics Commission said there was only "some" rise in standards between 1995 and 2000.

BBC News, February 18, 2005

PISA Results Show Need for High School Reform

America's 15-year-olds performed below the international average in mathematics literacy and problem-solving, according to the results from the Programme for International Student Assessment (PISA). The test, given in the spring of 2003, assesses the abilities of 15-year-old students from 41 countries (including 30 of the most developed) to apply learning to problems with a real world context.

U.S. Department of Education Press Release, December 6, 2004

Student Test Scores Faltering, Failing in Major States, New Government Data Reveal

SACRAMENTO, CA—Children's reading scores have stalled or declined in the nation's largest states since Congress passed the No Child Left Behind Act in 2001, according to data released by governors and state school chiefs.

U.S. Newswire, October 7, 2004

Test Scores Improve in City Schools

WASHINGTON—For a nation hungry for good news about its schools, some promising results are emerging where they are least expected: large-city school districts.

While reading scores for fourth graders are dipping nationwide, they are on the rise in such cities as Atlanta, Chicago, Houston, Los Angeles and New York. Some urban districts are even starting to exceed the performance of suburban schools on certain test scores, when students are sorted by demographics and race.

Christian Science Monitor, December 18, 2003

City's School Services Improving

BRADFORD—Bradford's education service has been rated as "satisfactory" in its latest Ofstead inspection. The city's education provision had been severely criticized in the past with inspectors labeling it unsatisfactory. Following the highly critical inspection report three years ago a private firm, Education Bradford, has overseen the city's schooling provision.

BBC News, March 24, 2005

(Continued)

Figure 3.1 (Continued)

> ### Hawaii's Top Principals
>
> Seven of Hawaii's best principals got rare pats on the back yesterday when they were named as finalists for the $24,000 Masayuki Tokioka Excellence in School Leadership Award.
>
> Research shows that school leaders play a crucial role in school success, and principals are under intense scrutiny these days as federal law demands constant improvement in student scores.
>
> *Honolulu Star-Bulletin News,* March 27, 2005

silently brainstorm answers and have all members of the group put their answers on sticky notes. Going in a clockwise fashion, group members voice their answers and place their sticky notes on a piece of chart paper used for the group. The cycle continues until there is a round in which everyone passes. Each group then takes a few minutes to review.

The group can then organize all of the information on the sticky notes into some kind of schema on the chart paper. Finally, each group has a spokesperson explain and post the schema. It is essential that those pieces of chart paper be posted where staff can see them, such as the faculty lounge, to demonstrate that they are valid and will form the basis of future discussion.

This exercise not only lets teachers explore why it is important to use data or evidence in school-based decision making, but it also makes them part of the process. They have explained why the use of data is important, and the posted schema demonstrate that they do indeed see why it is important.

Using the Three Dimensions of the Principal in Convincing Staff

In the role of leader, the principal can help convince staff of the validity of data-driven school improvement through actions such as these:

- Exhibiting passion about seeking and using evidence
- Modeling evidence-based decision making

- Being able to answer questions about the use of evidence
- Being able to answer questions about worldwide trends to accountability

In the role of professional developer, the principal can help convince staff of the validity of data-driven school improvement through actions such as the following:

- Providing the above-mentioned activities for staff to engage in discussion about the use of data in education
- Providing information about the use of educational data
- Being a resource or providing resources about data and school improvement planning

In the role of communicator, the principal can help convince the school community of the validity of data-driven school improvement through various actions, including the following:

- Constantly using data in communications to faculty, students, parents, and the community
- Explaining the use of data in educational accountability in local, district, state, national, and international forums as important

This modeling by the principal will also assist in convincing staff, students, parents, and the community that data-driven school improvement is the only clear, demonstrable way to ensure student success.

WORKING WITH LEADERSHIP TEAMS

Leadership teams, particularly in large schools, are an invaluable asset in implementing change. Their composition will vary, depending on the school or in response to the initiative being led, but their role is always to assist the principal in implementing lasting change. For example, if an initiative involves working with the community and service clubs to build a gymnasium, the leadership team would include a leader from the community, leaders from service clubs, and a leader from the physical education department of the school.

A leadership team in a high school might consist of department heads; in a middle school, it might consist of representatives from grade teams or subject teams; and in an elementary school, it might consist of representatives from each instructional division.

Much like the composition of leadership teams, the selection process varies by need. When the principal needs to hear the views of faculty, the community, or certain departments clearly, the members may be selected by their peers. At other times, they may be selected by the administration for their skills in a certain area or their leadership qualities. Sometimes both methods may be combined. In all cases, the selection criteria must be communicated clearly. In the case of leading data-driven school improvement planning, members of the leadership team must be capable of understanding, leading, and explaining complex change and, perhaps most importantly, must have credibility within the school, especially with other faculty members.

How Are Leadership Teams Effective?

Leadership teams can take the abstract and make it happen. They have the ears of their colleagues; they understand the culture and nature of their school; they are advocates for the initiative; and they can shoulder a lot of the work in designing, altering, and implementing effective change. Once the leadership team understands the process of data-driven school improvement planning, they can design appropriate strategies to develop and implement the process within the school. Using their experience, support from administration, and the feedback they receive from the faculty, they will run the process effectively.

Leadership teams require two essential supports to reach their full potential. Professional development is needed to explore fully the initiative they will be leading. As experts, they will be the ones to whom the school community looks for answers and the ones plotting the implementation. These teams also need the time to discuss the initiative, how it will fit into the school environment, the possible roadblocks, and what is already in place. From those discussions will come a valid and specific implementation plan based on the needs and culture of the school.

The principal should be a member of the team and should act as leader, professional developer, and communicator. The leadership role is one of providing the team with a framework and guidance based on policy, vision, district direction, and so on. The professional development role is facilitating the members of the team to gain the knowledge and skills they will need to lead the initiative. The communicator role consists of letting the school community know what the team is doing and why.

MAKING DATA USE EXPLICIT

As was demonstrated at the beginning of this chapter, all members of the school community constantly and consistently use data to inform decisions. Data can be found in more places than just externally imposed student assessments, such as those mandated by No Child Left Behind in the United States and Programme for International Student Assessment (PISA) and the Education Quality and Accountability Office (EQAO) in Ontario, Canada. What are report cards, for example, but summaries of data about student achievement in classrooms? We already have a culture for the use of data in every school; we just haven't begun to take advantage of it.

The principal's challenge is to demonstrate how evidence is used every day in making decisions in the school and, while not discounting the importance (or reliability) of externally imposed student assessments, see them as only a piece of information in the big picture. Here are some methods of doing this:

- The principal explicitly articulates the data used in every decision.
- Teachers explicitly articulate the evidence they have used in reaching decisions.

After a while, it will be evident that each and every decision made in the school rests upon some kind of evidence, that the culture of the school is already one of data-based decision making, and that explicitly basing school improvement on evidence is just a short step. Almost every decision, whether small or large, immediate or strategic, is based on input of some kind, and most of that input comes in the form of data. Consider the three cases from the daily routines of three schools described in Figures 3.2, 3.3, and 3.4 and consider the information used in making the decisions in each case. These are just a few instances of how schools work with data every day to help students succeed.

Figure 3.2   Vignette 1

Sam Johnson

It was about 10:15 AM when the call came to the office from Gillian Parsons's room.

"Somebody needs to get up here quickly," cried the obviously distressed voice. "Bill Rector hit his head on the floor and is bleeding badly."

By the time Susan Lowe, the principal, reached the room, Bill was sitting up, looking rather dazed, with a bloody T-shirt pressed to the back of his head. Susan asked Bill what happened. He replied that when he went to sit down in his chair at the start of the class, somebody pulled the chair away, and he had crashed to the floor. He didn't remember what happened after that until he had come to, lying on the floor bleeding with Ms. Parsons at his side.

After ascertaining that Bill had no injuries other than the cut and bruising on his head and a rather sore tailbone, Ms. Lowe had him taken to the office for first aid. His father was called and said that he would be there in a few minutes to take his son for medical attention. In those few minutes, Bill retold his story, but added that he was sure that he thought that Sam Johnson had been the person who pulled the chair out.

Bill's dad arrived. He rushed over to his son and asked what had happened. Bill reiterated his story, again blaming Sam. As he walked his son out of the office, Mr. Rector looked at Ms. Lowe and stated, "As soon as I'm through at the doctor's, I'm coming back, and you better have dealt properly with that bully Sam Johnson. This is not going to go away."

Susan knew full well that the district's Code of Conduct stated clearly that if one student assaulted another student and the victim "required the services of a qualified medical practitioner," the perpetrator faced immediate suspension and an investigation that could result in expulsion. This, indeed, was not going to go away; it was going to take a lot of time in her already overcrowded schedule.

She called Sam down to the office and asked him to tell what had happened.

"Well," said Sam, "I guess it was my fault. I was walking by Bill's desk, and someone shoved me. I lost my balance, put my hand out, and knocked his chair away just as he went to sit down. He fell—he landed on the floor and fell back, hitting his head."

"Are you sure this is how it happened?" Susan asked.

"Yes."

"And who pushed you?"

"Don't know."

"Did anyone see this?"

"Well, most of the class was there, but I don't think that most of them saw what happened. Khan Nguyen was close to me, and so was Holly Dunham, but I don't know if they saw anything, either."

Susan interviewed Khan and Holly. The former claimed to have been close to the action; the latter stated that all she saw was Sam pushing Bill's chair and Bill crashing down. She could not tell whether or not Sam had done it on purpose, but she thought that he did not, because it would have been unlike him. Both girls stated that Luis Gonzales and Abraham MacDonald were also witnesses.

By afternoon, Susan had interviewed almost all of the students in the class. All agreed that the starts of Ms. Parson's classes were not orderly and that there was a lot of "horseplay" going on in the room. Although stories varied on details and some students had seen nothing, nobody had seen Sam deliberately move Bill's chair. Furthermore, nobody knew of any animosity between the two boys.

At that point, Mr. Rector stormed into the office, demanding to see Ms. Lowe. When informed that she was with a student, he paced about the outer office until she was free. He entered her office and stood.

"What have you done to that Johnson kid?" he demanded.

"I'm afraid I can't tell you that," Susan replied.

"Well, let me tell you. Bill was in emergency at Holy Cross for four hours. He needed ten stitches to close up the split at the back of his head, and now I have to wake him every few hours all night to see if he has a concussion. You'd better suspend that Johnson kid for a good long time for what he did to my Bill."

Susan explained that she had been investigating the case all day, and that, although there were not a lot of witnesses, it was beginning to appear that Sam had accidentally knocked Bill's chair over.

At that, Mr. Rector exploded with rage. He began screaming at Susan, calling her incompetent and threatening to take the case to the police and to her boss.

Susan calmly replied (though her heart was pounding) that his tone was inappropriate and that she was ending the conversation at this point, although she would contact him the next day. She also stated that unless he left her office at this time, she would have him removed.

Mr. Rector turned and stormed out of the office, slamming the door so hard that the whole office shook.

In Vignette 1, "Sam Johnson," it would have been easy for Susan to cave in and discipline Sam Johnson severely, but she would have been unjust to do so. Although the initial evidence pointed to Sam's guilt, further investigation did not prove anything conclusively. The investigation did give Susan information with which to make her decisions about discipline; certainly she had enough information to know that she would not proceed to expulsion. She also knew that she would base her decisions on what actually happened, not on conjecture, and that her decisions would be defensible.

Figure 3.3   Vignette 2

Algebra

Ruth had taught Grade 8 math for years and considered herself a good teacher. Over time, she had moved from a curriculum that was based almost solely on computation to a balance of numeration, geometry, data management, algebra, and measurement. Her teaching style had gone from being the "sage on the stage" to "the guide on the side," and she was proud of the problem solving and mathematical communication skills of her students.

Yet these kids were struggling with math in Grade 9, so her principal arranged a meeting with Lech, the head of the math department at the neighboring high school, and a Grade 9 teacher.

The day went well. Ruth was surprised that the teaching of math in high school had changed as much as her own teaching had, and she noted that, in terms of pedagogy, the students were getting much the same approach in Grade 9 as they had in Grades 8 and 7. After observing three classes, Ruth and Lech sat down in the staff room over coffee and chatted. Almost at the end of the conversation, Lech produced his course outline. Almost immediately, Ruth mentioned that almost the whole course seemed to deal with algebra and that there was no component of geometry.

"That's because we don't deal with geometry until Grade 11," Lech stated.

"But I spend three months on geometry," Ruth exclaimed. "Is that a waste?"

From the investigation, Susan also now knew that the root cause for this incident was the disorder at the start of Ms. Parson's class and that she would have to find a way to help the teacher make the entry to her class safer.

In Vignette 2, "Algebra," Ruth discovered that she was spending a great deal of time on an area of mathematics that students would not revisit for two years. This information helped her reshape her course. She cut the amount of time devoted to geometry by over a half, concentrating on making sure students comprehended the big ideas, rather than dealing with the detailed information. She utilized the time created to reinforce the computational, problem-solving, and communicational ideas underlying algebra in the Grade 8 curriculum. The next year, when they met, Lech was happy to inform Ruth that her students had found a much higher degree of success in the ninth-grade mathematics courses. The use of process data (what was taught) had informed an instructional decision, which impacted on student success.

Figure 3.4   Vignette 3

Spotlight on Co-op

At a secondary school, teachers were finding it more and more difficult to place co-op students. Employers were increasingly telling the school that they were just too busy, too understaffed to be mentors—or just not returning calls.

Frustrated, the principal invited personnel from businesses that had withdrawn from the program for a series of working lunches at local restaurants. At the lunches, members of the co-op department first asked the employers to share their experiences with co-op students and then got down to why their business was no longer participating. At first, the conversations centered about excuses, but gradually it became clear that the real issue was the huge amount of paperwork required to register a co-op student, the size of the weekly report, and the complexity of the summative evaluation and discharge. Another issue was that businesses felt that they received no credit for working with students.

A small committee was formed to worked on the problem, streamlining all the paperwork and arranging for a weekly "Spotlight on Co-op" column in the weekly paper.

Co-op opportunities grew and continued to grow.

In Vignette 3, "Spotlight on Co-op," the feedback from local employers caused the school to revamp the paperwork involved in the co-op program and publicize the employers who participated. Not only did the program grow, but the working lunches, soon involving employers, school staff, and students, became a fixture and helped shape the program. The local chamber of commerce began to sponsor a summative "Employment Breakfast" involving students, teachers, and employers to celebrate co-op in the community and, especially, to celebrate the employment successes coming from the co-op program. The program was more than rescued.

Each of these cases demonstrates how evidence, carefully gathered and thoughtfully considered, can lead to good decision making in a school. Whether it is discipline, instructional practices, supervision for safety, scheduling, or making courses more effective, good collection and use of data informs effective change and thus student success.

SUMMARY

The principal must nurture the growth of data-based school improvement, and if it is to take root, this growth will take time. It must be tailored to the needs of the school, and each step must be carefully planned, with time given for the introduction of material, the digestion of material, and the incorporation of material into the existing culture at every step.

The first step is convincing school staff that data-driven school improvement is positive, possible, and valid. The principal has a role as leader, professional developer, and communicator in this area and must constantly model passion about and use of evidence, know why data are essential in school improvement, and envision how the process to make this happen will occur. Leadership teams are one very effective method of implementing change: These teams are made up of credible staff members who, once given the professional development necessary to make them knowledgeable and skillful in the area, can provide leadership to take the rest of the staff through processes to implement improvement in the school.

Most decisions made in a school are based on some kind of information. Therefore, schools already have a culture of data-based decision making, but most do not realize this. Through explaining the evidence behind each decision, the existing data-driven culture can become explicit, paving the way for a culture of data-driven school improvement. In the next chapter, we will look at how the collection of data, already a feature of all schools, can be formalized, made more complete and comprehensive, and be shaped for analysis to inform school improvement.

C H A P T E R 4

Finding Reliable, Valid, and Comprehensive Data

Traditionally, schools have been driven by "hard" data, such as standardized test scores; pass/fail rates; graduation rates; postgraduate employment statistics; state, province, or district test scores; and results from competitions such as science fairs. On a broader scale, the news media in particular like to compare "home" scores, as a matter of local pride, against the scores of other districts or countries on international tests such as PISA. Such comparisons, especially if they are negative, often drive political agendas. Likewise, employers want data to show that a school or district is producing graduates equipped to enter the workforce.

Educators, on the other hand, realize that while the measure of student achievement is very important—in fact, maximizing such achievement is the goal of every educational institution—such success is not possible without ascertaining the best possible pedagogy, then aligning school structures and resources to support such teaching and learning. To do so requires much more evidence than is found in the "hard," summative data. The net must be cast wider and deeper to improve the process of education so that student achievement can be improved.

Knowing that students are reading below expected norms in a school simply indicates that improvement is required; only an analysis, using different types of evidence, can demonstrate how learning experiences can be changed to support and guide students better in their acquisition of reading skills.

Schools and communities are rich mines of such information. But to glean the gold that will aid in effective decision making from the dross that will cloud and confuse, the administrator must be aware of the available types of information, which type or types will be most useful in any given situation, and where to search for that evidence.

TYPES OF DATA

It is important for school communities to recognize and use the four main types of data:

- Outcome
- Demographic
- Process
- Perceptual

Each is valuable, and each describes certain areas, but none can stand alone. Schools tend to focus on outcome evidence, as it is readily available and is easy for staff and parents to understand, but the context provided by demographics, processes, and perceptions is essential to interpretation of the "hard" numbers. Similarly, outcome and demographic data are generally quantitative or number based and, thus, easier to "crunch" into easily understandable charts and graphs, while process and perceptual data are often "qualitative," with narrative and anecdotal strands that are hard to put into numbers yet provide the background the numbers cannot show.

Outcome Data

The first and most obvious type of data is outcome data. This is information that is observable, measurable, "hard" information, often summative, and it usually comes in the form of numbers. The following are examples of outcome data:

- Marks on report cards
- Results from standardized tests
- Promotion/retention rates
- Failure rates in individual courses
- Course enrollment rates
- Rates of suspension/infractions

This type of data abounds in schools. It is fairly simple to collect and easy to present, making it the type of evidence most used in educational settings. Outcome data highlight successes and failures; these data do not, in most cases, indicate how to change what happened. Outcome data are almost always quantitative information: easy to express in numbers, percentages, charts, and graphs. Because it is easy to visualize, such information appears to be easy to understand and, thus, is very powerful. It is often difficult to realize that it does not tell the whole story. The drawback is that this evidence is only about the end product; it does not address how that result was achieved.

Imagine an automotive assembly plant. Inspectors check the completed cars coming off the end of the line and find that 0.6 percent have paint flaws. This is important data for managers in the plant, especially as they know that fixing paint flaws is very expensive and that a competing factory in another country has a 0.05 percent paint flaw rate, lowering its final costs. But the data do not tell those managers how to improve the paint process. To do that, they will have to examine the product from the paint booth to the end of the line; determine where and how the flaws are caused; and then, through research, modify the production process at the point or points of difficulty to improve the paint on the cars.

Outcome data, as in this case, often pinpoint an issue or a success, but more information is required to find why the issue or success happened.

Demographic Data

Demographic data provide the principal with powerful tools that can be used to inform teaching. The easiest such evidence to collect is quantitative. For example, census returns will give you family income ranges, ethnicity, proportion of the population with languages other than English spoken at home and what those languages are, and so on, but it is important to remember that the information is based on all families in the area, not just those who populate your school. School-based surveys can give you the same information in a more detailed and relevant way for some dimensions (though certainly not for income level). This, combined with numbers you already have in your school (number of students who have repeated one or more years, absenteeism, number of students on free or reduced-price lunches, and so on) can draw a strong quantitative picture.

This is evidence about people, and it is the kind of information that can inform school administrators about the makeup of their school. Demographic data are most often obtained from censuses or from well-designed surveys. Following are examples of demographic data:

- Percent of students in a district/school for whom English is not the first language of the home
- Socioeconomic status in a defined area
- Levels of formal education in households in an area
- Availability of social services in an area
- Languages spoken by students in a school
- The mobility of families in an area
- Staff age/gender

An example of how demographic data were used to influence student learning profoundly can be found in a large urban center in Ontario, Canada. As in many industrial cities, the core has gradually decayed as heavy industries moved out and suburbs were built. Elementary schools in that area, as evidenced by their registers of attendance, have a very high rate of mobility, up to the point where in a school of 300, 450 students will be coming in and going out every year. Furthermore, when the schools began tracking students, they found evidence that confirmed the beliefs of teachers and administrators that these students never left the city; they just moved from school to school within the core as their parents were regularly evicted and found new rental units. Outcome evidence also showed that these students had large gaps in achievement, especially in mathematics and science.

School personnel from all of the inner-city schools met to discuss the issue and reasoned that, as there was a smorgasbord of curriculum expectations at any grade level and teachers addressed these expectations in different orders, kids moving from school to school in any year were probably addressing some expectations many times, perhaps once in each of three schools, but not addressing others at all. Such gaps could accumulate over many years, especially in an area such as mathematics, where one concept builds on another so that without a firm foundation, progress gradually slows almost to a standstill.

The solution was to divide the curriculum expectations into monthly units. All teachers in Grade 5 in the inner city would address the same expectations in September, for example, so that the learnings would be the same at every school. Since students generally moved at month's end, teachers reasoned that this division would work. And it has. Outcome data have demonstrated general improvement in mathematics since the project was launched.

Another elementary school, built in a rapidly expanding suburban area, used demographic data to inform instruction in quite a different way. The school library was poorly equipped, so teachers routinely assigned homework that required research outside the school as part of the curriculum. They were finding that this homework was often incomplete or not done at all.

Demographic data revealed that the community consisted predominantly of two-income families, most of whom commuted to a city about an hour's drive from home. In addition, a significant minority of families lived in subsidized housing, working at poorly paid jobs or living on social assistance. Furthermore, the closest public library was over two miles away, and the community had no public transit whatsoever.

The implications were that most children were either in day care or home alone before and after school; that the public library was inaccessible for most children; and that, although many families were connected to the Internet, a significant minority could not afford to be connected and, thus, could not do research online.

The solution was to offer afterschool access to the school's computer lab for Internet research and to limit library research to in-school times with what resources were available at the school. Outcomes in research-based achievement improved, especially for those students without Internet access at home.

A walk through your school's neighborhood can tell you much about your demographics. Simply looking at the housing can give you a good grip on the socioeconomic level of the community. Checking for available services (library, medical facilities, parks, government offices, public transit, etc.) can inform opportunities for community partnerships, as can watching where children congregate. Students spend most of their time in their community, outside school, and it is important to know that community. Such qualitative data cannot be expressed in numbers but are extremely important.

Similarly, interviews with students (at a middle school or high school level) or their parents about their cultural backgrounds and what that means to their schooling can be extremely valuable qualitative data, data definitely worth pursuing to round out the picture of the demographics of your school.

Process Data

This type of data describes how things happen in your school—the only area over which your school community truly has control. Process data describe how students are instructed in your school, from the individual to the group, the class, the division, or department to the whole school. These data include how decisions are made about what is taught, how it is taught, who teaches what to whom, and how schedules are built. They describe instructional processes, assessment practices, decision making, and other processes. They are information about how your school does business.

This information is almost always qualitative; it tells a story and usually cannot be well expressed by numbers or bar graphs. It is best described in narratives and flow charts. These data are generally anecdotal in form and are often found in policy documents or in observations. Following are examples of process data:

- Observations of instructional practice
- Running records of achievements for students
- Descriptions of how students/staff are involved in decision making
- Observations of the relationships among assessment, evaluation, and reporting in an individual classroom
- Policies about dispute resolution
- Practices in the distribution of the school budget

- Raw data of observations for teacher performance appraisal
- Descriptions of how the raw data become a final performance appraisal document

Process data can be sourced from many areas: administrators' reports; school improvement plans; and observations by administrators, department heads, and teachers. Senior students can be an excellent and crucial source of such information, as can parents, especially for describing communication flows between home and school. As each process is described by each of its stakeholders, triangulation of the evidence occurs, giving a balanced picture that is more valid and reliable than information from a single source.

A wonderful example of the collection and use of process data occurred in a family of schools implementing a comprehensive literacy program. This involves providing a language-rich environment as the context for explicit skills instruction. It includes reading aloud, modeled reading, shared reading, guided reading, and independent reading, as well as modeled, shared, guided, and independent writing taught in the context of vocabulary building and word study. Implementation involved learning about and using very specific techniques, such as a word wall, leveled readers, and so on. After about a year of implementation, the principals created a process based on a balanced literacy chart (see Figure 4.1 on page 52). In each school, teachers were asked to sit in interdivisional groups at a staff meeting. They were asked to fill out the chart independently and then share their work with a partner, then with the group, and finally with the whole staff.

The outcomes were manifold. Primarily, each teacher reflected on his or her practices in the process of teaching literacy. They each then had the opportunity to share and engage in professional dialogue with another teacher from another division, so primary teachers shared their practices with middle school teachers and so on. Finally, the whole group came up with a range of practices that could work at various grade levels but shared common foundations, as well as a list of available resources, shared definitions, and a wish list for further resources. The teaching of balanced literacy became a shared practice, based on common beliefs and actions through a sharing of the process data.

Another example of the use of process data (also referred to in Chapter 2) comes from a small middle school. In this case, the processes were the school timetable and instructional practices.

Figure 4.1   Balanced Literacy Chart

Process Data

Literacy Instruction Term	Definition	How much time (on average) per day?	Resources I have to support it	Resources I need to support it
Word Wall				
Guided Reading				
Shared Reading				
Literature Circles				

Teachers in this school were trying to shape instruction to meet the needs of the students, as described in the current literature and as they found students in their school. After much reading and discussion, they decided that science and mathematics should be taught together to strengthen the cross-curricular learnings inherent in the two subjects; that English, history, and geography should be taught together for the same reasons; and that the arts, including physical education, music, visual arts, drama, dance, and second languages, should be taught by specialists. They also believed, based on research, that students should have large blocks of learning time and should have as few different teacher contacts in a day as possible.

When they tried to turn these beliefs into a timetable, it became evident that the optimal day would be divided into thirds. This way, each student would learn math and science in a single classroom from a single teacher for a third of the day; English, history, and geography in a single classroom from a single teacher for a third of the day; and the arts in specialized classrooms from specialized teachers for a third of the day. This did not match the current school process, which used two recesses and a lunch break to divide the day into four unequal parts. Two large blocks of time were provided (before morning recess and following afternoon recess), but the third block was fragmented by the lunch break.

The staff was so convinced that the timetable had to be changed that they lobbied the administration, the district, and the community to change the school day to consist of three equal blocks of instruction, broken by two "nutrition breaks." The new process was adopted and demonstrably increased learning in all areas.

Perceptual Data

This type of data describes what people believe. It is a description of processes, institutions, evidence, and people as viewed by specific audiences. Perceptual data are almost always qualitative: It is narrative and uses words rather than numbers to describe a situation. Perceptual data are often linked to beliefs and values and are usually seen as reality by the person or group expressing them. Following are examples of perceptual data:

- The results of parental surveys about bullying in a school/class
- Opinions solicited in a focus group about the image of a school/district
- Editorials
- The results of student surveys about safe/unsafe places in a school
- The results of surveys about how a school/district communicates with various audiences

Many educators have had the experience of sitting down, perhaps to a meal in a restaurant, and overhearing people nearby verbally assassinate a teacher or a school. That is perceptual data at its purest. It is an adage that, if you want to find out what the community thinks about your school, all you need to do is attend a hockey/football/baseball practice in your community, especially if the only thing parents have in common is the sport and the school their kids attend. And who has not had the phone call that begins with, "I was just talking to a group of people in the community, and . . ."?

How people perceive something is often as important as what it is. Politicians are very aware of this and constantly poll their populations to find out what people believe, not what they know. Legislation is often based on meeting perceived needs, as evidenced by polls and focus groups.

School and district administrators gather perceptual data every day. Parents call or visit, students are heard, and letters arrive complaining about (and, rarely, praising) teachers and processes. While this is evidence, it may well not be valid or reliable. Administrators hear regularly from a small portion of the parent community and spend much of their time working with a similarly narrow segment of the student community. This does not give a broad view, as it does not include the famous "silent majority," whose views may differ radically from those heard by the administrator on a daily basis.

An example of perceptual data is views about bullying. Perhaps because *bullying* has no clearly accepted definition, perceptions tend to vary widely. What is perceived as bullying by one student or one parent is seen as "horseplay" by another student or parent. Students who are accused of bullying by other students often claim that they are really the victims, because their actions are truly reactions to harassment by their accusers. Little is clear.

Some districts or schools have created surveys to gain evidence about how students, parents, and staff perceive issues, such as bullying, in a building or district. Because perceptions of such issues tend to be personal and colored by experiences, beliefs, and values, the survey must be fairly large and cover a wide and representative demographic of the district or school population if it is to be valid and reliable. When all stakeholders are asked their perceptions, triangulation of data can occur. This means that when most or all of the stakeholders hold a similar perception, that view is widely accepted and, thus, is reliable and valid as evidence. Survey questions must be designed to be neutral and specific (Have you witnessed another student being bullied at school in the past three months?) rather than vague and leading (Is bullying an issue at your school?). Such surveys, like many seeking perceptual data, are best designed by experts; otherwise, the information gained may be unreliable due to the wording or structure of the instrument.

Yes/no answers do not get at perceptual data, which are, by nature, narrative. Surveys attempting to find such evidence must give opportunities for the respondents to write narrative comments to flesh out their reactions. This quantitative data is essential and is often more relevant than the rating scales in the survey.

Yet in spite of the difficulty of obtaining valid, reliable perceptual data, such data are powerful information, as they describe the way that people are thinking about something. How people think governs their actions, and this type of evidence often explains why people are acting the way they do and leads to plans to change a perception, which will change the action.

All four types of data can inform decisions in a school. In some situations, one type is more relevant than others, but educators should always consider seeking all four types to ensure sound decision making. Each type of data offers a view of one dimension of the issue, with the richness of that type of data determining the resolution of the view. The more types of evidence that are considered, the more dimensions of the issue become visible. Collecting multiple types of data increases the probability of success in addressing the issue. Some further examples of the four types of data are given in Figure 4.2 on page 56.

It is also important to remember that information is not defined by how it is displayed but by what it reflects. For example, the cultural profile of a school resulting from a survey concerning attitudes toward bullying, the components of a staff meeting, and marks distribution for physical education in a Grade 4 class could all be displayed in a pie graph format. The first example is demographic data, the second is perceptual, the third is process, and the fourth is outcome. Each is displayed in the same manner, but the content and type of information they reflect is quite different.

INTERSECTING DATA

To be valid, information must come from the reality of the school, and such reality, to paraphrase Oscar Wilde, is rarely plain and never simple. Often a single issue may have dimensions of two or more types of data. In fact, "crossing" two types of data can provide much deeper insight into the school; see Figure 4.3 on page 57 for some examples.

The richer and more complex the issue, the more types of evidence are involved. Three or even all four types may intersect. Looking at the intersections of three types of data enables you to see trends, check on whether initiatives aimed at specific segments of the population have worked, and understand how a teaching methodology works from both a teacher's and student's perspective.

Figure 4.2   Examples of the Four Types of Data

Type of Data	Examples
Outcome	✓ Results of state testing ✓ Results of standardized tests ✓ Course means and medians aggregated or by classroom ✓ Reading inventory scores by grade, division, or school ✓ Results in district competitions ✓ Percentage of students successfully enrolling in college/university
Demographic	✓ Number of students by grade, division, or subject ✓ Education level of adults in the school catchment area ✓ Social services available in the local community ✓ Number of students in whose home English is not spoken ✓ Percentage of students transferring in or out throughout the year ✓ Number of dropouts
Process	✓ What parts of a balanced literacy program are successfully running? ✓ Is science taught experientially or by lecture? ✓ How do decisions about the Code of Conduct get made? ✓ What is the staffing process for the school? ✓ How are parents involved in the life of the school? ✓ How are school accounts kept?
Perceptual	✓ Where do students feel unsafe in the school? ✓ Do parents feel there is a bullying problem in the school? ✓ Do staff members feel heard at staff meetings? ✓ Do staff members feel that the budget allocation process is fair? ✓ Do parents feel that this school prepares their children well? ✓ What do students feel that the school does best?

Figure 4.3   Some Benefits of Intersecting Data

Types of Data	Examples
Demographic Outcome	✓ Comparison of student grades and attendance ✓ How do students from homes where English is a second language compare academically with students whose home language is English? ✓ Does the number of credits in the first two years of high school predict whether a student will drop out?
Demographic Process	✓ What strategies do Grade 2 teachers use to teach reading to English-language learners? ✓ How does the school communicate with parents who do not speak English? ✓ How are economically disadvantaged students assisted in obtaining school supplies?
Demographic Perceptual	✓ Is there a gender difference in whether or not students perceive the school as being safe? ✓ Are older students happier with their experience at the school? ✓ Do less experienced staff members see the rest of the staff as mentors?
Outcome Process	✓ Has the introduction of a balanced reading program improved reading scores? ✓ Do gender-discreet classes increase student grades for both genders? In all subjects? ✓ Does ability grouping in a math program increase student success?

The intersection of all four types takes into account how specific categories of students prefer to learn and whether those processes are effective, or how specific groups of teachers like to teach and how those processes are effective. For instance, in Figure 4.4 on page 58, the following information must be collected:

- Identifying mature, returning students
- The attendance of students in the subjects and grades involved, both for the whole student body and for mature, returning students
- The attitudes of mature students and the whole student body about regular attendance
- The achievement levels of mature students and students as a whole in the affected subjects

The information should be gathered separately (disaggregated) and then looked at as a whole through the home and expert group process. Each member of the "home" group becomes the "expert" on one piece or sector of the data, then returns to share what he or she knows with the others in the "home" group, each of whom has similar expert knowledge of one piece or segment of information. Through sharing and discussion, the larger picture painted by the evidence becomes clear, without each member having to look in depth at all the information available. But before this process begins, each member of the group seeking answers to the question must be thoroughly familiar with each type of evidence.

Figure 4.4   Multiple Data Dimensions

Types of Data	Examples
Demographic Perceptual Outcome	✓ How do parents of English-language learners perceive standardized testing, and do these perceptions influence the results of their children on those tests? ✓ Do students who participate in extracurricular activities have a better attitude toward school, and does this influence their marks?
Demographic Process Outcome	✓ Do remedial math vocabulary classes help English-language learners get better grades in mathematics? ✓ Does aligning the sequence of math instruction in inner-city schools result in better math marks for students with high mobility?
Process Outcome Perceptual	✓ Do a teacher's views on the best way to teach reading in Grade 1 influence that teacher's methodology in approaching student literacy, and does this influence students' progress in reading?
Outcome Demographic Process Perceptual	✓ Do boys' attitudes to books differ from those of girls in Grade 5, does that difference influence the way they participate in reading programs, and does their participation influence their progress in reading? ✓ Do returning, mature students in high school have better attendance because they are choosing to go to school, and does their attendance influence their achievement?

An example of how a school used the intersections of different types of data to increase student success, as cited by Bernhardt (1998), can be found in a large elementary school in Southern California.

Demographically, 42 percent of students were members of minority groups, 40 percent spoke languages other than English, and 36 percent received free or reduced-price lunch. The outcome data were found in the results of standardized tests and on measures that identified whether or not students were meeting grade-level standards, and process data were gathered about the teaching of reading.

To begin, the staff broke down test scores by demographics, intersecting the two types of data. It was discovered that students not fluent in English were having the greatest difficulty in reaching grade levels in reading. Teachers then spent more time with these students and soon realized that the root cause of their difficulties in reading were that they had poor word comprehension.

Based on this finding, instructional processes were changed: Newly arriving students went first to specialized classrooms where they received intensive work on word concept skills, then to a reading intervention program, before being integrated into the "regular" reading program. The reading scores of the students from limited-English backgrounds soared, and the gap between those learners and students from English-speaking backgrounds narrowed.

DEFINING DATA TYPES WITH YOUR STAFF

All staff members in a school need to deal with evidence; the principal cannot be the sole person dealing with the data that will be used to drive the school plan. If staff members are not involved, they will not and cannot participate meaningfully in the decision-making process; thus, they will not fully accept any outcomes or plans. The principal needs to teach the other members of the school community how to find and deal with data if authentic decisions are to be made.

Figure 4.5 demonstrates to staff members that evidence is all around them; that finding it does not involve difficult searches; and that they can, in fact, find relevant data fairly easily within their own environments.

Staff, students, and parents must be made aware of the types of data that can help them understand how to begin collecting balanced evidence about an issue. But having the information is not

Figure 4.5   Samples of Data by Type

Samples of Outcome Information

Test Results

State testing	International testing
District testing	Tests from teacher manuals
Teacher-made tests	Standardized tests
Exemplars	

Performance Assessment

Portfolios	Summative tasks
Reading assessments (DRA, First Steps)	Displays
Musical performance adjudication	Sports team records
Science fair projects	Formative assessment

School Sources

Report cards	Course pass/fail rates
Number of suspensions	Reasons for suspensions
Office referrals	Dropout rates
Code of Conduct	Students in leadership programs
Social work referrals	Police contacts
Public speaking competitions	

Samples of Demographic Information

About Students

Number of students in the school	Class sizes
Enrollment in specific courses	Absences/lates
Number of honor students	Retention rates
Graduation rates	Course pass rates
First language	Language spoken at home
Number of special needs students	Mobility rates
Gender	Lunch status (free/reduced)
Part-time employment	Participation in extracurriculars
Health issues	Attendance at preschool

About Staff

Age	Experience
Special qualifications	Hobbies
Previous employment	Gender
Type of certification	Additional qualifications
Rate of participation in professional development	

Number of teachers/
paraprofessionals/support staff
Mobility rate   Projected retirement rate

About the School
History   Special courses/services offered

Grade levels offered   Special classes offered

Rate of bussing   Special equipment

About the Community
Urban/suburban/rural   Socioeconomic level

Level of education of adults   Percent of population renting

Support agencies available   Economic basis

Growth or shrinkage projections   Crime rates

Samples of Process Data

Instructional Processes
Types of instructional strategies   Grade/subject teacher teaming

Strategies for special needs students   Long-range planning

Types of assessment by grade/division   Reporting practices

Planning processes   Teacher appraisal processes

Student grouping practices   Instructional review practices

School Organization
Staffing process   Scheduling process

Creation of Code of Conduct   How the timetable is created

How community services are accessed   How district services are
                                                 accessed

How students are placed in classes   How teacher roles are assigned

Professional Development (PD)
How staff accesses PD   Participation rates

How PD is directed   Relevance to school goals

Frequency with which PD is offered   Incentives for PD

Resources
What is the budget allocation process?   How are course loads adjusted?

What is the support staff allocation   How is time allocated?
   process?

How are community services accessed?   How are raised funds allocated?

Students
How do students register?   How do students change courses?

How are extracurriculars organized?   How are sports teams chosen?

How are student leaders chosen?   How are the voices of students
                                                 heard?

(Continued)

Figure 4.5 (Continued)

Samples of Perceptual Data

Community Perceptions

What is the school best at?	What is the school worst at?
Is the school day appropriate?	What are the students like?
Is the school part of the community?	Is the school accessible?
Are children safe at the school?	Does the school communicate well?
Do the students achieve well?	Are students happy at the school?

Parent Perceptions

Is my child happy at school?	Does the school prepare my child?
Do the teachers communicate with me?	Is my child safe at school?
Does the school tell me good news?	Do the teachers like my child?
Is enough homework being given?	Is my child progressing?
Is the school well enough funded?	Is the school day appropriate?

Teacher Perceptions

Am I supported by administration?	Do my peers support me?
Is it possible to do my job well?	Is the school on the right track?
What do I need to be a better teacher?	Is the community supportive?

Student Perceptions

Am I safe at school?	Are there bullies at school?
Does my teacher like me?	Where do I turn for help?
Will this school get me where I want to go?	Is school relevant?

---

enough; they need to be able to use data effectively to shape the planning, implementation, and review processes. See Figure 4.6 for an exercise that staff or departments can use to practice safely the data-driven school improvement planning cycle. Because the information in this exercise is "neutral" and has no emotional baggage, they will be better able to concentrate on the process. This provides these same teams with an understanding of the flow of the cycle before approaching the more emotional issues related to their own data.

Figure 4.6   Activity to Help a Group Understand the Types of Data

Getting staff and community involved is the first and, often, the most difficult step. This activity is an easy yet very effective way to get them involved through a highly participatory exercise. The content may not be that used here, although this content is "neutral" in that it comes from well-accepted research and is not connected with any particular school, so issues of ownership do not muddy the waters.

This activity gives participants (staff, parents, or students) the opportunity to do the following:

- Brainstorm sources of evidence related to a school issue.
- Look at the type of each source they have selected.
- Recognize the depth and breadth of evidence available.
- Choose the most relevant sources, based on stated criteria.

Most importantly, working through this exercise will give the participants the opportunity to safely work with data, getting a feel for looking for relevant, balanced data. It can be used in a staff meeting, a school council meeting, or any similar environment to introduce participants to the four types of evidence and to let them use their knowledge.

Because this activity involves the transmission of knowledge, the facilitator (who may or may not be the principal; knowledgeable people from the staff or from the community can lead this activity) must be familiar with the types of data, as outlined above.

The facilitator first needs to define briefly the four types of data. The pages dealing with both the definitions and the samples of each type of data could be used as handouts. Once these are understood, the participants need to apply what they have learned. To do so, they can then be introduced to a set of goals. For the adventurous, this could be some of the goals of the school plan, but this is site-specific and involves ownership, which may cause some distortion. For a safer start, one might use the effective schools correlates.

The activity is based on the 1966 study by the Equal Educational Opportunity (EEO), which concluded that schools do not make a difference—that solely the home environment affected the achievement of children. In response, other researchers looked at schools where all children, especially minority and disadvantaged children, were achieving at or beyond curricular expectations. They asked why and how these schools made a difference and if their success could be replicated in other schools. The researchers set out to isolate and describe the critical factors that set "effective schools" apart from schools that had similar demographics but were not nearly as effective in terms of measured student achievement. Over the next decade, the amount of research grew, and the findings were codified into seven correlates of effective schools:

(Continued)

Figure 4.6 (Continued)

1. A safe and orderly environment

2. A clear, focused vision for learning

3. A climate of high expectations for success

4. A focus on high levels of student achievement

5. Frequent monitoring of student progress

6. Instructional leadership

7. Strong home-school relations

The researchers also found that none of the above correlates stands alone. In fact, when a school demonstrates improvement, all of the correlates are present and interconnect to create a culture and climate that result in student and school success.

A fuller description of each of the correlates can be found in the "Educator Toolkit" section at the back of the book (Resource B: Characteristics of Effective Schools). For further information, please see Lawrence W. Lezotte's *Correlates of Effective Schools: The First and Second Generation* (1991).

Each correlate has a set of indicator. For instance, the indicators for a Safe and Orderly Environment are as follows:

- A behavior code emphasizes respect, self-discipline, positive relations, and the prevention of inappropriate behavior.
- Student discipline is fair and equitable.
- Students of all ages take leadership roles.
- Behavior policies and expectations are understood by and communicated to parents, students, teachers, and all staff.
- Students work together to maintain a safe environment.
- Programs are in place to address issues such as conflict mediation, bullying, and building healthy relationships.

The participants as a large group are shown these indicators of a Safe and Orderly Environment and are asked to brainstorm data or evidence that would demonstrate how present each of these indicators is in a school. The workshop leader or an assistant scribes these sources on chart paper or on an overhead.

When the brainstorming abates, the group is asked to identify each source as outcome (O), demographic (D), process (Pr), or perceptual (Pe) data, while the instructor marks the type beside the source on the chart/overhead.

At this point, the group, led by the instructor, should examine the relative proportions of the various types of evidence—that is, whether or not the group has relied too heavily on one type and if any type is underrepresented. Often, groups unaccustomed to using data will look almost exclusively at outcome data, such as the rate of suspensions, average number of incidents involving police in a month, or the number of leadership opportunities for students. A discussion could ensue about why all types of data are important and how, for instance, the perceptual data found by asking random persons in a hallway about the behavior policies and expectations in the school is really the only way to gauge if such policies and expectations are understood by parents, students, teachers, and all staff.

The next step is to begin to realize how much evidence can be collected about any aspect of a school.

For this exercise, the participants are divided into groups of three to five. There are two methods of doing this exercise, depending on the size of the room and the number of participants.

Method 1: This method is best used with groups of 12 to 30 who are seated at larger tables, one table per group.

Each group is given one of the six correlate charts (see "Educator Toolkit") posted to a piece of chart paper and one or two markers. Remember that they have already done a Safe and Orderly Environment, and it cannot be used again in this exercise. To begin, each group has about five minutes to read the correlate and to write on the chart paper some sources of information about the indicators, noting the type of data from each source.

After five minutes, the groups pass the correlate and chart paper on to the next group, who reads the information, then adds further data sources (and their type).

The passing of the charts continues again, until the available time is used or each group has written sources of data for all the correlates. The time needed for each group to fill in further sources will decrease as the exercise moves on, and each group does not need to deal with all correlates; three or four will suffice.

Method 2: This method is best used with groups of 25 and up or in rooms where the participants are seated at small, individual work areas and there is room to move around the walls.

Chart papers, with the six correlates attached, are posted on the walls. If the group is especially large, two or three copies of each correlate can be posted, but the entire six correlates must be posted in a single area, with another six being posted in a separate area and so on. The number of charts posted must be equal to or slightly greater than the number of groups.

(Continued)

Figure 4.6 (Continued)

Each group is given markers and moves to a posted correlate. To begin, each group has about five minutes to read "their" correlate and to write on the chart paper some sources of information about the indicators, noting the type of data from each source.

After five minutes, the groups move to the next posted correlate and chart paper. They read that correlate and the sources of data noted by the previous group, then add further data sources (and their type).

The cycle continues until each group has both read and given sources of evidence for all six correlates or until time dictates the end of this part of the exercise. Again, the amount of time required at each station will decrease as the exercise moves along.

Conclusion

After the final turn, the charts are passed one more time (or the groups move to a final posted chart). Each group now has to decide on the three listed sources of data from the chart that would best demonstrate the presence of the indicators and report to the whole group why they chose those sources.

At the conclusion of the activity, the participants should have a good grasp of the four types of evidence and have had the opportunity both to find many sources of information about specific outcomes and to prioritize them into a meaningful yet manageable collection of data.

Another great tool can be found in Figure 4.7. This exercise is designed to get team members familiar with using all four types of data by looking for particular types of evidence in their own environment and envisioning how each type of data could be both useful and important in data-driven decision making.

SUMMARY

When most people think of data in an educational setting, they think of test scores, report cards, school rankings (the British "League Tables," for example), and so on. While this kind of information may be useful, it is neither deep enough nor broad enough to be a valid, reliable, comprehensive start to the school improvement process. A much broader scope is needed than the "slice of time" snapshots provided by such testing, and a deeper view into the culture of the school is also needed. These may be accessed by collecting a range of data.

Figure 4.7   Exercise 2: Using Different Types of Data

Another exercise in using different types of data to improve student success is found in *The Handbook for SMART School Teams* (2002). In this exercise, the leader/facilitator creates a number of cards about sources of evidence.

Perceptual Data: In-Depth Interviews

Definition: One-on-one conversations using open- and closed-ended questions

When to use it:

1. To identify and learn about issues and concerns in depth
2. To understand the full range of perceptions

Perceptual Data: Surveys

Definition: A set of questions that asks people about their opinions, usually written but can also be conducted by phone

When to use it:

1. To quantify concerns identified through interviews or focus groups
2. To understand the perceptions of large numbers of people

Process Data: The Evaluation Form

Definition: A set of questions or statements about a school's programs, instructional strategies, assessment strategies, and classroom practices for students and staff

When to use it:

1. To keep track of in-school processes to document progress
2. To build a continuum of learning for students and staff

Process Data: Literacy Evaluation Form

Definition: A set of questions or statements about the school's literacy programs, including instructional strategies, assessments, and classroom practices for students and staff

When to use it:

1. To keep track of in-school processes and document progress
2. To build a continuum of learning for students and staff

(Continued)

Figure 4.7 (Continued)

Demographic Data: Community Cultural Profile

Definition: Description of the culture of the students, staff, school, and the surrounding community as well as the context within which the school operates

When to use it:

1. To create or modify a school-to-home communication plan
2. To help design curriculum delivery practices to meet the needs of the community

---

Demographic Data: Staff Profile

Definition: Description of the teaching experience of the staff through a questionnaire

When to use it:

1. To help target professional development to the whole staff and sectors of the staff
2. To develop suitable mentorship pairings

Each group takes a card and fills out a sheet or chart paper to answer the following questions, based on the data collection tool on their card:

How Can We Use This Source of Evidence or Data to Improve Student Learning?

Name of the tool:_____

Type of data:_____

What kinds of evidence would you expect to collect using this tool?

What are the advantages of using this tool?

What are the disadvantages of using this tool?

After the groups have finished, they share their findings.

To participate fully in the school improvement process, teachers must be aware of the different types of data so that they can consciously use as many types as possible when gathering information to inform the plan. Simply marshalling outcome data will not inform an effective plan. Teachers (and community members who may be involved in the school improvement process) must learn about the types of data and where they can be found, as well as how intersecting data can become even more powerful. Once the staff is aware of the four types of data and the importance of using all four and, if possible, using intersecting data, then they can begin to work on the data-driven school improvement plan.

In the next chapter, we will explore the process of data-driven school improvement planning and suggest an exercise to get faculty and community members to attempt the process in a risk-free environment.

CHAPTER 5

The Data-Driven School Improvement Planning Cycle

How often has a sheaf of data been dropped in front of you with the question "Well, what do you make of that?" Sometimes school faculties feel the same way. Results from the latest statewide testing arrive in a bundle, and the superintendent is asking this question. Often the answer is a result of a hurried, hunch-ridden, holistic intake of as much undigested information as possible, usually with few checks for validity or reliability.

The school improvement planning cycle is a much more effective process for dealing with evidence, one that ensures that the information speaks for itself. It is an organized, thorough approach to using evidence effectively to inform school planning. This method involves having groups, such as staffs or departments, examine information carefully and without bias, to use their findings to create a targeted and accountable plan, then continually check the implementation of that plan for effectiveness.

THE SCHOOL IMPROVEMENT PLANNING CYCLE

As an example, your school team has decided to focus on issues with student performance in mathematics. You, as an administrator, have supervised the collection of many types of data, and now you have information about student performance by gender, grade, department, teacher, strand of the curriculum, ethnicity, and attendance. You have gathered the team to analyze the data and to create a plan to deal with the issues that emerge. However, instead of simply handing them sheaves of information, you can take them through the school improvement planning cycle:

1. Predict

2. Check assumptions

3. Observe the data

4. Interpret the data

5. Plan

6. Gather further data

7. Repeat the cycle

See Figure 5.1 for a visual overview of the school improvement planning cycle. This visual helps to demonstrate the sequence of events and provides a reference that can be followed as each step is explained fully below.

As an example of how a school team can work through this cycle, we will use the example of a secondary school with significant failure and dropout rates. The staff felt that one of the best predictors of student success was regular attendance, so they decided to look at attendance patterns in the school. Office staff collected all the attendance data for the past school year and then disaggregated it by time of day, course, teacher, grade, and age. Without distributing the information in any way, the leader began the cycle.

1. Predict

The first step in the process is to ask the group to predict attendance patterns. What will they look like? Will there be a pattern based on

Figure 5.1 School Improvement Planning Cycle

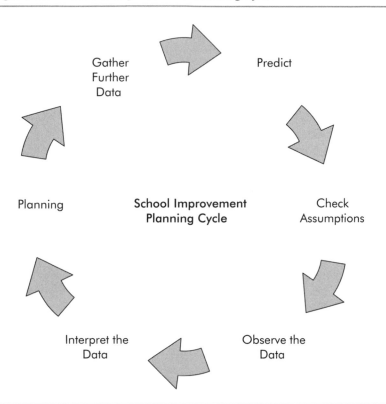

- times of the day;
- days of the week;
- times of the year;
- particular courses;
- particular teachers; or
- student gender?

In this part of the cycle, the group is given information that will be self-analyzed to lay bare any biases or assumptions the group may have about the issue (in this case, attendance).

2. Check Assumptions

Look over the answers the group gave. Why did they make these assumptions? Are underlying issues causing the group to distort the data? At this point, biases and assumptions need to move from under the table to out in the open; otherwise, they will distort the interpretation of the data.

In our example, the group may have predicted that boys will have more attendance issues than girls and that there would be more absenteeism in the afternoons. The assumptions behind these predictions could be as follows:

- Girls are more compliant than boys.
- Girls are better socialized to school than boys.
- Students get bored with school as the day progresses.
- It is hard for students going out for lunch to return to school.

It is essential to understand these assumptions so that the group is aware that they may color the interpretation of the real data they are about to see. Without recognizing their own biases, they will see the information through the lens of their assumptions, and the data will be distorted.

3. Observe the Data

This is the most difficult phase of the cycle, and it has to be handled with care. Do not overwhelm the team with many related but different pieces of information; only look at one piece at a time or divide the group into teams and have each team look at one piece.

The critical part is that the group or team looks at the evidence and discusses only what "pops out" as information—no assumptions, no excuses, no rationales, and, above all, no interpretations. This step is pure observation: What do you see? What do the data show?

At this phase, the leader needs to prompt the group or teams with critical questions, such as the following:

- What patterns can you see?
- Is there an evident trend?
- Do you see anything that surprises you?

The discussion should be summarized in writing. The leader also must try to ensure that assumptions or opinions (the leader's or the team's) do not cloud the observation. At this point, group members need to ask themselves what else they need to know. Again, to use our example, the data may show relatively even patterns of attendance but that

- absences rise throughout each semester in every grade;
- absences are highest in Grade 10, slightly lower in Grade 9, much lower in Grade 11, and lowest in the graduating year; and
- absences in English and math classes are higher than in all other classes in Grades 9 and 10.

The group may also ask for more information on the intersection of poor attendance and academic failure, especially in Grades 9 and 10.

4. Interpret the Data

As the group begins to interpret, or to put the evidence in context, it is important first to look for celebrations or victories. What do the data show us is happening well? What does this demonstrate that we are good at?

At this point, the data must be placed in the bigger context of the state, the province, the district, the community, the school, the department, and the classroom. The group must understand that, no matter how vital, this information is only a piece of the puzzle—that there is context and it is usually in the interaction of the context and the evidence that discussions must happen. This, however, is not the time to blame; it is the time to keep focused on the facts and what they tell us.

In our example, the interpretation may well be that students in Grades 9 and 10 who are not doing well academically, especially in the core areas of English and math, tend to be absent more than other students, until the point where they drop out of school entirely, usually toward the end of Grade 10.

5. Plan

In the interpretation phase, the group decided on the victories and the issues. In the planning phase, they must begin to look at how to build on the strengths to remedy the weaknesses.

To use our example again, the group may well begin planning how to engage students who are failing academic courses in Grades 9 and 10. This may involve increased counseling for students at risk, the development of remedial courses in which students can experience success, or other strategies.

6. Gather Further Data

After the plans are complete, the group will look at what data will be needed to see if the plan is succeeding and create the instruments to collect that information.

To go to our example again, the group may devise a tracking system for the attendance of at-risk students in Grades 9 and 10, as well as the general attendance data that will continue to be captured.

7. Repeat the Cycle

And the process begins again.

When the cycle is fully integrated into the fabric of the school, teachers will go through the cycle with students as they hand back assignments or give out reports, using questions such as these:

- How do you think you did?
- Why?
- Let's look at the (test, assignment, report). Is anything here a surprise?
- What did you do well? What wasn't so good? How does this fit with what you generally do?
- How can you improve for next time?

IN-SCHOOL APPLICATION AND PRACTICE

Spring training in baseball or training camp in football allows experienced, talented players to relearn skills and to practice them before going into game action. Similarly, a person wishing to play competitive chess first learns the rules, then practices, before attempting to play against more skilled players.

The progression of learning rules and skills, practicing them, and then applying them is a foundation of education, and we must use that process when training groups to deal effectively with data. We have learned the rules: the four types of data and the cycle for using data. Now it is time to practice.

Tempting as it is to rush to the application stage, where the group will work through the cycle for using data with real evidence from their own school, that is as dangerous as putting a football player who has never scrimmaged into a game. Just the practice of the cycle is difficult enough; adding the emotional overtones of using evidence that has real and important meanings can make the first time through the process overwhelming.

It is probably best to use neutral, fictional material for the first practice, as the participants will have no emotional ties to the material and can, thus, deal with it in a clean, "clinical" way, much as a football player practices tackling or blocking on teammates to learn proper technique rather than in the heat of a game, where emotion can overcome skill.

In the "Educator Toolkit" section at the back of the book, you will find two case studies (Resource C: Case Study—Elementary and Resource D: Case Study—Secondary) presenting data for secondary and elementary educators. Each consists of a page of overall information about a school followed by five pages of additional data. While these schools are fictional, they are based on real schools and form a useful set of evidence from which to work.

The Practice Activity

In this activity, "home" group members will have a chance to look at the overall information for a school and individually reflect on the predictions they would make about school results and on what assumptions they made those predictions. They will then meet with an "expert" group to look at another piece of data about the school, observing that information. Finally, they will go back to the home group, where information from all the expert groups will be shared along with assumptions, the entirety of the evidence will be observed and interpreted, and plans will be made. Each participant will experience the whole data use cycle.

Again, the facilitator or leader of the activity could be the principal or another skilled facilitator chosen from the staff or the community.

Home Group

Home groups have (ideally) five participants. Of course, it is not always possible to divide workshop participants into groups of five, but the leader should keep as many groups as possible at five, with the final group then consisting of between five and nine members.

Everyone in each group is given the first page of overall information about the school. The principal or facilitator then asks that each participant individually write down the following:

- What they would predict, in general or specific terms, about this school
- What assumptions they are using to make these predictions

Expert Group

Each of the five other pieces of data about the school from the case studies is placed in an envelope, numbered 1 through 5. Each envelope is then placed on a separate table or in a separate area.

The leader then asks each group to number off, 1 to 5. The last and largest group, the only one with more than five members, may have two 1s, two 2s, etc. The number 1s from each home group are then directed to envelope 1, the number 2s are directed to envelope 2, etc. They are not to open the envelopes yet, but within their new "expert group," they are to discuss the following:

- What each had predicted about the school
- On what assumptions those predictions were made

When that discussion is complete, they may open the envelope and observe the data. They will then do the following:

- Look at the information as a team and describe what they see, with no interpretations.
- Look for and describe what seems to "pop out" or what patterns the information shows.
- Discuss what seems surprising or unexpected.
- Discuss what other information will be needed to interpret the data.

Home Group

When that discussion is complete, the participants return to the home group. There they will do the following:

- Share the information they have each learned.
- Discuss what the information, as a whole, tells them.
- Discuss what plans should be formulated to improve the school.
- Formulate further questions.

An excellent method to set the tone for discussion of data and to ensure that every member of the home group gets to be heard is the round robin. In this strategy, each person gets to contribute one piece of information, and then the next person gets to contribute, in turns. The talk goes around the table until everyone has shared all of their data, with members passing if they have shared all of their evidence before other members are finished.

When all the data are shared, the technique is repeated as each member of the group, in turn, contributes possible interpretations about the evidence they have heard. This again continues until all interpretations have been heard, with participants passing if they have nothing else to say before other members are finished.

The final round robin is one in which group members contribute possible solutions to the issues raised by the information, following the same format as in the first two steps. The group may then debrief and talk about their feelings and learnings in going through the cycle.

They should now be ready to work with real data, but as in the old adage from the dawn of the computer age, garbage in gives garbage out. How can the group be sure that the evidence they are working with is not garbage?

ENSURING THAT EVIDENCE IS VALID AND COMPLETE

Seeking balanced, relevant evidence and processing it through the data use cycle is long, hard work. It would be discouraging, to say the least, to find that all that work was in vain—that the data were not useful and, because of that, the group had "put its ladder up against the wrong wall" and the school was not progressing.

To avoid this, the principal must ensure that teams know how to distinguish relevant from irrelevant data interpretation. A useful tool to help a team know they are on the right path is the four Cs: Complete, Consistent, Comparable, and Concealing.

Complete

Do you have the complete picture? Lotteries sell tickets by advertising what it would feel like to be a winner. They do not mention the odds of winning (usually poorer than the odds of being struck by lightning). They conceal the almost overwhelming odds that a ticket buyer will never be a grand prize winner. The picture they paint is wildly unlikely to happen, and if the real data are taken into account, buying a ticket in the hopes of experiencing the grand prize–winning ecstasy depicted in the ads is an irrational act.

Large-scale assessment represents a "snapshot" in time. Data represent a frozen moment, not a "movie" of improvement over time. That frozen moment may or may not reflect the reality of achievements in each individual child or classroom. The child being assessed may have just suffered a tragedy, the class may have been taught by a succession of short-term teachers, or (the lottery winner) the class may have freshly learned a single concept being tested. It is also wise to consider the context:

- Classroom teachers' assessments and report cards
- Smaller (e.g., district) assessments using local norms as references
- Running records, such as First Steps and the Developmental Reading Assessment
- The context of the assessment (Had there been changes of classroom teachers? Was there a lot of sickness? Was there political protest by parents or teachers?)

When using surveys, was the number of respondents great enough to be considered representative of the population as a whole? Were demographics considered? Were the special, demonstrable characteristics of the school or district considered?

Incomplete evidence easily leads to false conclusions; consider the story of the four blind men trying to describe an elephant by describing only what each could feel at one time.

Consistent

Are there any surprises? Are the results from different sources about the same target consistent? Are results what you thought they would be? Consider consistencies with respect to the following:

- Individual students
- School results
- Past experience

Comparable

What are you comparing? Be sure your comparisons are relevant—you can only compare apples with apples. You can compare the following:

- Norms
- Subgroups
- Similar schools
- Standardized test results
- Identical surveys
- Census figures
- Results from dissimilar processes aimed at the same outcomes

When making comparisons, you must consider what might have changed:

- Teachers
- Programs
- Students (you can't compare this year's ninth graders with last year's ninth graders!)
- The nature of the assessment
- The environment of the assessment
- How the data are reported

Concealing

What is being hidden? This is the most difficult, yet the most powerful, source of disinformation to discover. If you looked at the value of shares on the New York Stock Exchange over time, you would see great variability in the yearly values. Through the 1920s, for instance, share prices rose steeply. This attracted many people to invest in shares, as they believed that they could double their money quickly. This decision ignored the long-term trend of slow, steady growth and culminated in the crash of 1929, when prices tumbled badly. Similarly, share prices in the 1980s and early 1990s rose much more quickly than was the historic norm, and again, this time through mutual funds that advertised only the returns of the immediate past rather than long-term growth figures, people were induced to buy, only to find a steep decline in prices. Looking at the short term, rather than the long term, led to poor decisions.

We must always be aware of the big picture and gather enough evidence to be sure that what we are looking at is complete, consistent, and comparable and is not missing vital data. Only then can we be sure that when we plan, based on the data, it is highly likely that we will make good decisions.

NEXT STEPS

The data cycle is an appropriate and excellent tool for dealing with data and, in most situations in schools, there is no need for other tools. Some educators, however, may wish to refine their use of evidence using further tools. While in-depth statistical analysis or the creation of controlled studies is well beyond the grasp (or need) of most school groups, some enhancements to the process are possible.

Once a group is comfortable with using the data cycle, new and more sophisticated techniques can be used to enhance the process. There are many techniques: Two important ones are triangulation and the problem solution frame.

Triangulation

Put simply, triangulation is using more than one observer, location, theory, or methodology to investigate an issue. By using several perspectives, it enhances the possibility of seeing the issue in deeper perspective and sharper focus. Like using two eyes instead of one, the method adds depth. It uses multiple observers, theories, methods, and empirical materials, and it has the following properties:

- It can be employed in both qualitative and quantitative studies.
- It is a method-appropriate strategy for ascertaining the credibility of quantitative analyses.
- It becomes an alternative to traditional criteria such as reliability and validity.
- It is a preferred methodology in the social sciences.

There are four basic types of triangulation:

- *Data triangulation:* Data are collected at different times by different persons and in different locations.
- *Investigator triangulation:* Data are collected by multiple, rather than single, observers.
- *Theory triangulation:* More than one theoretical scheme is used to frame the interpretation of the data.
- *Methodological triangulation:* More than one method is used to find or interpret data.

The possibility exists for "multiple triangulation," where the investigative group combines data from multiple observers, many theoretical perspectives, and many sources and methodologies. The richer and broader the data collected, the finer the grain of the picture that emerges.

The Problem Solution Frame

The problem solution frame (Figure 5.2 on page 84) is a graphic organizer that may help groups deal with the Interpret the Data and Planning phases of the data cycle. The innermost circle poses the question, and possible solutions are written in the surrounding bubbles. The group then discusses the possibilities, decides upon the one that seems to be the "best" solution, and writes it in the box below the organizer. There are separate organizers for the

Figure 5.2   Problem Solution Frame: Interpret

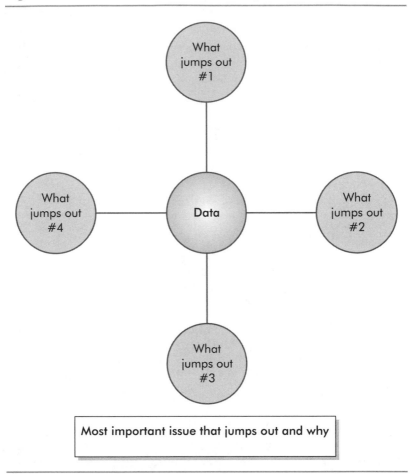

Interpret the Data and the Planning sections of the cycle, with the solution from the Interpret the Data frame becoming the center circle for the Planning section (see Figure 5.3).

A third problem solution frame (Figure 5.4 on page 86) can be added to move from the Planning to the Gather Data section of the cycle. Again, the solution from the Planning frame becomes the center of the Gather Data frame.

SUMMARY

The data-driven school improvement planning cycle is a useful way to move from a large aggregation of data about an issue

Figure 5.3   Problem Solution Frame: Plan

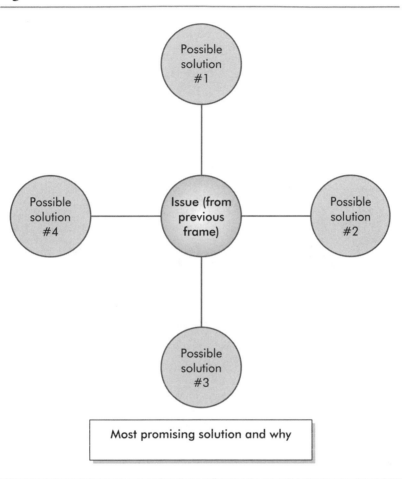

toward a solution and to check to see if that solution has solved the problem. It can be used at a school, department, or grade level or in a single classroom.

Implementing the improvement planning cycle in problem solving allows staff the chance to predict what the data will look like before they see the information and to discuss these assumptions before they even approach the evidence. This often allows the evidence to "pop out" at them differently than they had predicted. This method is also a great way to involve each member of the group as each examines one area of the evidence, so no one member is overwhelmed by the volume of the data but each area of evidence is seen. By working as a group

Figure 5.4   Problem Solution Frame: Gather Data

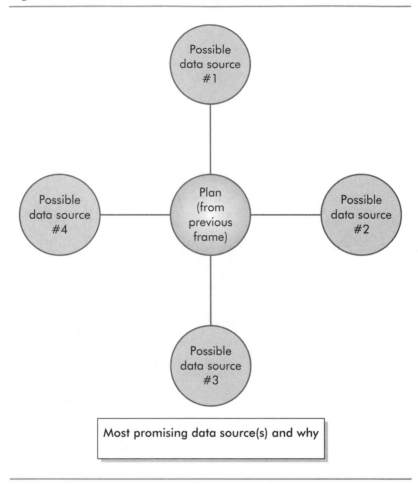

when approaching a problem, staff can better examine and interpret the evidence before moving on to possible strategies to create the needed improvements.

As school groups become more adept at the process, it can be refined by using more sophisticated techniques. In the final chapter, we will look at some refinements in the process that will become possible as the staff gets more used to the cycle and the aspects of the school plan get more specific.

CHAPTER 6

Embedding the Cycle in the School's Culture

D ata-driven school improvement planning, once properly initiated, becomes normal practice in a school, primarily because it works and is transparent to all. Sometimes, however, glitches can appear that either slow the process or, in extreme cases, cause it not to be effective. There are generally simple troubleshooting solutions for these. Another possibility is that teachers may wish to make the process more precise and to link it with SMART (specific, measurable, attainable, relevant, time-based) goals. This, too, is achievable and is a natural next step. Finally, staff may need assistance in finding research-based strategies for the improvements required by the findings of the process. In this chapter, we will examine all of these areas and look at the role of the principal as leader, professional developer, and communicator in facilitating refinements to the process.

FACILITATING SUCCESS

The school improvement planning cycle does not always go smoothly, even if it is introduced slowly and thoroughly. Common difficulties are poor or incomplete data, analysis and interpretation marred by assumptions, lack of appropriate strategies to implement, inability or unwillingness to change strategies, and inability or unwillingness to give up fruitless changes.

Poor or Incomplete Data

Gathering data is a balancing act: A team can spend so much time gathering the data that the whole process goes into paralysis, or they can gather too little data and be unable to make valid interpretations. Either extreme can derail the process. When gathering information, teams should ask themselves the following questions:

- Is the information valid and reliable?
- Have we attempted to gather all four types of evidence?
- Are we missing anything else that is essential?
- Does the information we have gathered look at all angles of the issue?

Teams also need to realize that though incomplete data will create an invalid plan, it will be corrected by a need for more data later in the cycle, so the issue is self-correcting.

As leader, the principal should be asking the above questions about the data until they are internalized by the teams. He should provide monitoring of data collection, either personally or through leadership teams, intensively at first as the teams hone their skills in this area. As professional developer, the principal, either in person or through leadership teams, should provide support for effective data collection. This may be training, time, money, or other resources, but it is essential to the success of the improvement. As communicator, the principal must let others in the school community know what the team is doing and why they are being provided with resources.

Analysis or Interpretation Is Flawed by False Assumptions

Assumptions, such as "kids living in poverty cannot learn as efficiently as others," can invalidate the analysis of information and skew interpretation. That is why the cycle starts with the Predict and Check Assumptions phases. It is essential that the group get their assumptions, usually hidden, out on the table so that all can acknowledge them and take them into account during the Observe the Data and Interpret the Data phases.

It is the role of the principal as leader to ensure that assumptions are revealed and are explicitly taken into account when dealing with the data. As professional developer, the principal must ensure that the team is aware of their assumptions and have the support both to understand and deal with them. As communicator, the principal should ensure that all members of the team hear the assumptions clearly.

Lack of Appropriate Strategies

Once an issue has been identified, the team must find appropriate strategies to deal with it. Lack of such research-based, up-to-date methodologies will result in the issue not being addressed and can stall the school improvement process.

The strategy search is the equivalent of a literature search in the development of a thesis, and the resources are similar. While the primary source is educational databases on the Internet, some districts, states, and countries have created research-based strategy banks. The National Reading Panel, for instance, has published *Teaching Children to Read: An Evidence-Based Assessment of the Scientific Research Literature on Reading and Its Implications for Reading Instruction* (2000) and other information available at its Web site (www.nationalreadingpanel.org). The U.S. Department of Education offers much information on its Web site (www.edu.gov), such as the *Foundations of Success: The Final Report of the National Mathematics Advisory Panel* (2008), a superb summary of research in the area of instructional practice in mathematics. State and provincial departments of education also offer informative summaries of research, such as the resources about boys' literacy on the Web site of the Ontario Ministry of Education (2008; www.edu.gov.on.ca). Districts may also offer such summaries, adapted to local use.

The principal as leader has the responsibility of ensuring that teams do appropriate strategy searches, then examine all of the possibilities before making a choice. As professional developer, the principal must make sure that the team has the time, guidance, resources (e.g., Internet access, printers, and ink), and assistance to gather the strategies, examine them, and make choices. As communicator, the principal must inform stakeholders of the process so that the choice of strategy is not seen as random.

The Difficulty of Change

While most teachers will embrace change to improve student performance (it is, after all, why they came into the profession), sometimes change can be difficult. Teachers may feel that new strategies denigrate what they have been doing in the past and, therefore, call their competence into question. They may feel that a strategy that research demonstrates is ineffective and should be replaced is part of what they believe in and, therefore, who they are. Letting go of what they have done (with what they perceive to be success) and replacing it with a strategy about which they are unsure (even if research tells them it is what they need) is a difficult process.

The principal as leader must recognize that change is hard for teachers. She should provide structures to support change while dealing with the phases that many faculty members will experience to different degrees while moving through the improvement process. She must understand that teachers, by changing their practice, are in effect changing themselves. As in any major change, the phases of disbelief and anger have to be experienced before the change is finally accepted and then embraced.

As a professional developer, the principal must support the change process both with emotional support (praise, encouragement, empathy) and with whatever information is needed. As communicator, the principal must communicate the rationale for the change clearly and constantly to all constituencies. A common instance of this is the weekly spelling list in an elementary school. While research has clearly demonstrated that such an activity has, at best, limited effect on student spelling and that well-rounded word study is far more effective, the Monday spelling list and the Friday test are part of educational culture for many parents (it is what they did) and many teachers. Ending the traditional program, thus freeing up 20 minutes of wasted time, is a difficult process for both teachers and parents. The principal must support both groups consistently through leadership, professional development, and communication if the change is to move forward. Leadership will involve working with staff to plan the change, with explicit time lines, including the removal of old texts and the provision of additional support as needed. Professional development will involve monitoring of the change, supplying relevant information, training, encouragement, financial support, and praise as necessary. Communication will involve, among other things, working with parents so they understand the rationale for the change, the process, and the results.

Another issue with change is the difficulty in dropping a new strategy that the data indicate is not resulting in the improvement it is meant to address. Sometimes a team has gathered data, predicted, checked assumptions, looked at the data, analyzed, interpreted, and selected a strategy based on what they have uncovered. They implement the strategy, then gather data to see if it is effective. Most of the time, the strategy is effective, but occasionally it is not and the data clearly show that. Obviously, it is not the right strategy for the situation and should be dropped, but the team has a huge time and emotional commitment to that strategy and often have great difficulty letting it go.

As leader, the principal must have the team recheck the data about the results of implementing the strategy. They must revisit their assumptions and try to look clearly and objectively at the information, then make a decision about whether the strategy is effective or ineffective, based solely on valid, reliable, comprehensive data. If the decision is to continue the strategy but to modify it to make it more effective, the principal then moves into the professional development support dimension. If the decision is to abandon the strategy, the principal must lead the team back through the data to search for a different research-based strategy, then again move into the professional development dimension to support that change. As communicator, the principal must clearly yet positively frame the reasons that the strategy was dropped or modified, based on the data, and inform stakeholders that new strategies will be implemented to continue to address the need.

Once the cycle has been used a few times, teams will become accustomed to collecting valid, reliable evidence that is as comprehensive as is necessary, taking assumptions into account when analyzing and interpreting and doing an appropriate strategy search. They will also learn to change strategies more quickly when the process tells them to do so and to become more flexible and research driven in their teaching practices. This means that, as the processes unfold, the principal's role as motivator, monitor, and mediator will gradually decrease, although it will never end. It also means that the leadership teams will be able to take on a more extensive role in those areas, reporting to the principal.

ADDING TO THE TOOLKIT

As schools gradually move to a data-driven school improvement culture, the process can be made more precise by adding more tools to the toolkit: getting to root causes and translating the plan into SMART goals. Both concepts hone the cycle by making it both more precise and transparent. The process of getting to root causes can eliminate many of the "red herring" distracters that are either out of the control of the school (and thus inappropriate for school action) or can be shown to be spurious. SMART goals cause a school to focus on effective short- and long-term strategies to reach achievable goals and to demonstrate that those goals have been met.

Root Causes

It is often difficult to pinpoint what causes an issue in a school. For instance, why are boys not reading as well as girls in Grade 3, or why are there fewer girls than boys enrolled in 12th-grade physics? Some teams will form hunches from the data, but this is really not helpful. If there are a number of possible causes, some must be eliminated to focus fully on those things that will make a difference. That process can focus on root causes.

Paul Preuss defines *root cause* as "the deepest underlying cause, or causes, of positive or negative symptoms within any process that, if dissolved, would result in elimination, or substantial reduction, of the symptom" (2003, p. 3).

To reach that root, we must also be aware that not every root cause may be within the circle of control or even the circle of influence of the team or the school. As Victoria Bernhardt (1998) has written,

> A problem is something we can do something about, so we can focus time and energy in the direction. A condition is something we cannot do anything about—we acknowledge it and go around it, but we do not waste time trying to change it. (p. 177)

We must focus on solving problems but only acknowledge conditions.

With that in mind, a method of getting to root causes is as follows:

1. The team brainstorms all possible causes of the problem. A good way to do this is for the group to apply sticky notes to chart paper.

2. Causes are categorized and organized by having the group move the notes following an organizational template (see Figures 6.1 and 6.2). See the "Educator Toolkit" section at the back of the book (Resource E: Brainstorming Organization Chart Template 1 and Resource F: Brainstorming Organization Chart Template 2) for reproducible copies of these templates that can be used to get the results noted in Figures 6.1 and 6.2.

3. All conditions outside the control or influence of the school (such as Internet access at home) are eliminated.

4. The team lists types and sources of data that would help find out whether this cause does indeed contribute to the problem.

5. The team members then seek those data and bring them back to the team.

6. If the evidence demonstrates that implementing strategies to remove the cause do not affect the major issue, that cause is not a root. For example, if the issue is poor mathematical reasoning in students, one cause to be examined may be the rate of use of calculators by students. However, changing that rate has never been shown to affect the level of mathematical reasoning, so it cannot be a root cause.

7. At that point the team examines the remaining causes against the indicators of a root cause:
   - You run into a dead end asking what caused the proposed root cause.
   - Everyone agrees that this is a root cause.
   - The cause is logical, makes sense, and provides clarity to the problem.
   - The cause is something you can influence and control.
   - If the cause is dissolved, there is realistic hope that the problem can be reduced or prevented in the future.

8. Root causes remain and can be dealt with through strategy search and implementation.

This is a lengthy and complex process, but if rigorously pursued, it will result in very positive results for the school improvement plan.

Figure 6.1   Brainstorming Organization Chart Sample

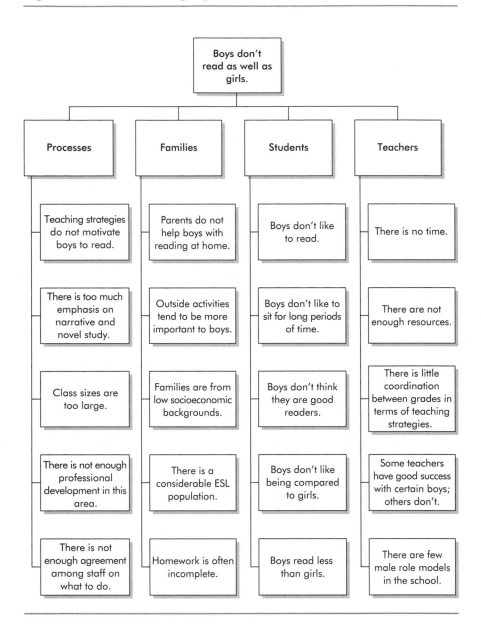

Figure 6.2 Brainstorming Organization Chart

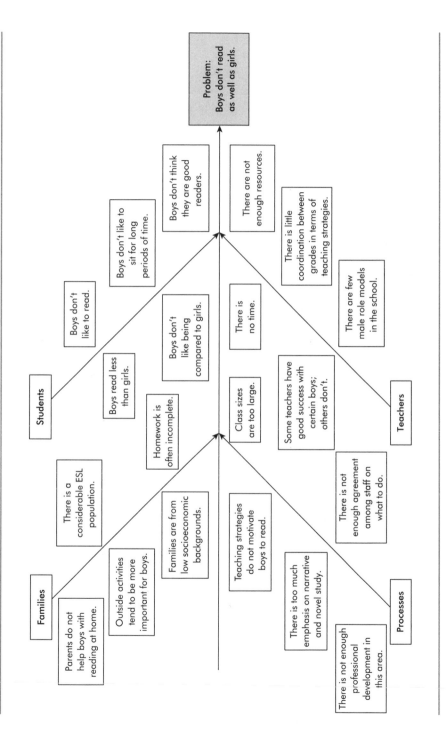

Using the Process to Build SMART Goals

SMART goals are

- **s**pecific;
- **m**easurable;
- **a**ttainable;
- **r**easonable; and
- **t**imely

Many jurisdictions are mandating that school improvement plans be couched in SMART format because it makes the improvement process much more accountable, as specified data must be collected at specified time points (usually fairly close together) to determine if the goal is being approached.

To begin, the overall goal must be formulated. As an example, we will look at a school where 34 percent of the boys are reading at grade standard in the sixth grade, while 68 percent of the girls are at standard. The data demonstrate that the school must deal with boys' reading skills. The overall goal will then be to raise the number of boys reading at grade level by Grade 6. The SMART goal takes this overall goal and rephrases it in specific, measurable, attainable, reasonable, and timely terms. The team may set the attainable, specific target that 44 percent of the boys will be reading at grade level in a year. The team decides that the measurement device will be the Developmental Reading Assessment.

Once a root cause or series of related root causes has been identified, the cause must be rephrased as a strategy. For example, a root cause for poor reading scores for boys might be that there is no appropriate reading material for boys in the classrooms or in the library. This would be reframed into a strategy that the school will create a library of reading resources for boys. Another root cause for the same issue may be that there is too much emphasis on the reading of novels. This would be reframed into a strategy that more time will be spent in the classroom on the study of graphic novels and manuals.

The team would then have to decide what the targets in each area will be. For instance, the target for the first strategy would be that there are at least 50 pieces of material specifically suited for boys' reading in each first- to sixth-grade classroom within a year and 250 pieces in the library. For the second, the target may be 100 minutes per week devoted to such studies in each classroom from the third to the sixth grade.

The next step would be to specify measurement devices for the implementation of the strategies. Both are fairly obvious and simple, the first involving counts of the new boys' reading materials in the first- to sixth-grade classrooms and the library, the second looking at day planners for all of the teachers from the third to the sixth grade and to decide on a date for such measurements.

If the specific measurements demonstrate that the strategies have been implemented and the overall goal of increasing the number of boys reading at grade level in the sixth grade has been reached, the outcome is positive. If the strategies have been met and the scores have not risen to meet the goal, the strategies may have been incorrect, and a new search for causes must begin. If the measurements show that the strategies have not been implemented and the scores have not met the target, there will be pressure on the team to implement those strategies quickly. If the measurements show that the strategies have not been implemented and reading scores meet the target, there must have been other causes, and somehow strategies have been implemented to meet those causes.

A principal wishing to implement SMART goal planning as a part of the data-driven school improvement planning cycle is advised to read Conzemius and O'Neill's *The Handbook for SMART School Teams* (2002) for further information.

SUMMARY

Once the data-driven school improvement process has been used successfully a number of times in a school and faculty see how powerful a tool it can be in improving student achievement, it rapidly becomes part of the culture of the school. As leader, professional developer, and communicator, the principal must ensure that the process does not get derailed, for once lost, the belief in data-driven school improvement will be hard to regain.

When the process starts to become embedded in the values of the school, the principal should work with stakeholders to hone and improve the process. Through the use of root causes and

SMART goals, teams can become much more focused on the details of improvement and will be able to demonstrate ever more clearly the progress that the school is making.

While the purpose of this book has been to provide the principal with the tools to begin an effective data-driven school improvement planning cycle, it is hoped that, as years go by and teams become more practiced, the process will become ever more sophisticated and effective, to the betterment of all students.

It is a lengthy process to have staff, students, and the community understand the need to use data to drive the decision-making process and to help them understand the four types of information; what complete, reliable evidence looks like; and how to use it in the school improvement planning cycle. It takes even longer to embed the effective use of data into the school culture and to build more sophistication into the cycle. But the results are amazing and evident to all. Doing so is perhaps the best use of time for any principal as leader, communicator, and professional developer, as it leads directly to student success.

Educator Toolkit

Resource A: Sample Quotes

"Education is what survives when what has been learned has been forgotten."

B. F. Skinner

"If you are planning for a year, sow rice; if you are planning for a decade, plant trees; if you are planning for a lifetime, educate people."

Chinese proverb

"Education is a progressive discovery of our own ignorance."

Will Durant

"Education is when you read the fine print. Experience is what you get if you don't."

Pete Seeger

"He who dares to teach must never cease to learn."

Richard Henry Dann

"Education is the most powerful weapon which you can use to change the world."

Nelson Mandela

" . . . no two people see the external world in exactly the same way. To every separate person a thing is what he thinks it is—in other words, not a thing, but a think."

Penelope Fitzgerald

"The question is how do we come together and think and hear each other in order to touch, and be touched by, the intelligence we need?"

Jacob Needleman

"An organization's results are determined through webs of human commitments born in webs of human conversations."

Fernando Flores

"There is more than a verbal tie between the words common, community, *and* communication. *[People] live in a community by virtue of the things they have in common; and communication is the way in which they come to possess things in common."*

John Dewey

"Faced with the choice between changing one's mind and proving that there is no need to do so, almost everybody gets busy on the proof."

John Kenneth Galbraith

"The real methodology for system change begins and ends with ongoing, authentic conversations about important questions."

Tony Wagner

"The final conclusion is that we know very little, and yet it is astounding that we know so much, and still more astounding that so little knowledge can give us so much power."

Bertrand Russell

"We live in a society that is data rich and information poor. While data are not information; translating fact to understanding means relating data to something you already know and can visualize."

Robert H. Waterman

"We wanted to make sure that a year's worth of instructions resulted in a year's worth of gains."

Brian Benzel, Superintendent,
Spokane (Washington) Public Schools

"Learning is not attained by chance; it must be sought for with ardor and attended to with diligence."

Abigail Adams

"All stakeholders take ownership and responsibility for our children's achievement. We are convinced that community engagement is necessary in order to progress."

Inez P. Durham, Superintendent,
Plainfield (New Jersey) Public Schools

"The fundamental purpose of any public engagement initiative is to channel a community's concern, apathy or anger into informed and constructive action."

Annenberg Institute for School Reform,
Reasons for Hope, Voices for Change, 1998

"If you don't listen to your community, you may make some assumptions that you are meeting their needs, but you are not. I find public engagement makes our decision-making easier; otherwise you are just guessing what the public wants."

Jane Hammond, Superintendent,
Jefferson County (Colorado) Public Schools

"I don't think you'll survive without engaging your public. The public has to be in public education."

Yvonne Katz, Superintendent,
Beaverton (Oregon) School District

"There are no secrets to success. It is the result of preparation, hard work, and learning from failure."

Colin Powell

Resource B: Characteristics of Effective Schools

A SAFE AND ORDERLY ENVIRONMENT

The school has an orderly, purposeful atmosphere free from the threat of physical harm.

	Sources of Data
✓ A behavior code emphasizes respect, self-discipline, positive relations, and the prevention of inappropriate behavior.	
✓ Student discipline is fair and equitable.	
✓ Students of all ages take leadership roles.	
✓ Behavior policies and expectations are understood by and communicated to parents, students, teachers, and all staff.	
✓ Students work together to maintain a safe school environment.	
✓ Programs are in place to address issues such as conflict mediation, bullying, and building healthy relationships.	

School Improvement Planning: A Handbook for Principals, Teachers, and School Councils • Education Improvement Commission. © Queen's Printer for Ontario, 2000. Reprinted with permission.

(Continued)

(Continued)

A CLEAR, FOCUSED VISION FOR LEARNING

Parents, staff, and students help create a vision that is focused on student achievement.

	Sources of Data
✓ The vision is championed by the principal, vice principal, and school council.	
✓ An action plan has been created to put the vision into practice. The action plan is understood by all members of the community.	
✓ Staff, parents, and students work towards shared goals that will improve student learning.	
✓ All staff, parents, and students are able to answer the question "What does this school care about most?"	

School Improvement Planning: A Handbook for Principals, Teachers, and School Councils • Education Improvement Commission. © Queen's Printer for Ontario, 2000. Reprinted with permission.

A CLIMATE OF HIGH EXPECTATIONS FOR SUCCESS

Staff believe, and demonstrate behavior that indicates, that all students can learn and succeed.

	Sources of Data
✓ Teachers' classroom practices and language reflect this belief.	
✓ Learning expectations are understood by all staff, students, and parents.	
✓ All teachers understand and use a variety of techniques to measure and promote student achievement.	
✓ Parents and staff believe that schools control the conditions for success (e.g., by insisting on high standards).	
✓ Academic success, citizenship, attendance, and other aspects of positive behavior are recognized and celebrated schoolwide.	

School Improvement Planning: A Handbook for Principals, Teachers, and School Councils • Education Improvement Commission. © Queen's Printer for Ontario, 2000. Reprinted with permission.

(Continued)

(Continued)

A FOCUS ON HIGH LEVELS OF STUDENT ACHIEVEMENT

The school emphasizes student learning, taking little time for activities unrelated to learning. Teachers strive to provide enriched learning experiences throughout the day.

	Sources of Data
✓ Students spend most of the day working on curriculum tasks.	
✓ Classroom instructional time is protected, with nnouncements and other interruptions kept to a minimum.	
✓ Teachers work with one another as a team.	
✓ Classroom resources address cultural diversity.	
✓ Parents and teachers understand what homework is and why it is given.	
✓ All students are given opportunities to improve academically.	
✓ Students are able to express the purpose of their learning.	
✓ All students are given opportunities to succeed.	
✓ Cocurricular activities offer students opportunities to achieve success outside of the classroom.	

School Improvement Planning: A Handbook for Principals, Teachers, and School Councils • Education Improvement Commission. © Queen's Printer for Ontario, 2000. Reprinted with permission.

FREQUENT MONITORING OF STUDENT PROGRESS

Student academic progress is measured frequently. A variety of assessment methods are used, and the assessment information is used to improve student learning.

	Sources of Data
✓ Teachers inform students and parents about expectations for students' work.	
✓ Teachers collect information about student progress on an ongoing basis.	
✓ Teachers communicate student progress to parents on an ongoing basis.	
✓ Parents are considered partners in their children's education.	
✓ Teachers understand the achievement levels as described in curriculum policy documents and apply these levels consistently.	
✓ Students and parents understand the achievement levels as well (i.e., the basis on which marks are assigned).	

School Improvement Planning: A Handbook for Principals, Teachers, and School Councils • Education Improvement Commission. © Queen's Printer for Ontario, 2000. Reprinted with permission.

(Continued)

(Continued)

INSTRUCTIONAL LEADERSHIP

The principal is the curriculum leader in the school.

	Sources of Data
✓ The principal demonstrates a commitment to accountability for student results.	
✓ The principal observes classroom activities on a regular basis.	
✓ The principal provides staff, school council members, parents, and other community members with the professional development/training they need to understand the curriculum and, in the case of teachers, implement it.	
✓ The principal ensures that teachers understand and implement a variety of assessment and evaluation measures.	
✓ Staff are expected to teach at a high level, and this expectation is communicated to staff, students, and parents.	

STRONG HOME-SCHOOL RELATIONS

Parents are partners in the school.

	Sources of Data
✓ Parents are involved in writing the school improvement plan.	
✓ The school involves parents in a variety of ways.	
✓ School council members discuss student achievement at their meetings.	
✓ The school informs parents about curriculum, assessment, and evaluation policies.	
✓ Parents feel welcome in the school.	
✓ Parents are involved in writing the school's homework and behavior policies.	
✓ Teachers and parents discuss student learning and progress.	

School Improvement Planning: A Handbook for Principals, Teachers, and School Councils • Education Improvement Commission. © Queen's Printer for Ontario, 2000. Reprinted with permission.

Resource C: Case Study—Elementary

School Demographics:

Kindergarten to Grade 8: 427 students

Split classes common in Grades 1–6

Location: Large suburban center

Number of languages represented in the school: 5

% of students and/or parents who have immigrated to the country: 17

% of students with primary language other than English: 10

% of students new to the school between September and June: 21

Number of years in the country:

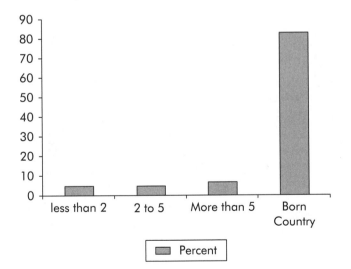

47 students (11% of population) are deemed exceptional (learning disabilities).

Curriculum

The school has a very active extracurricular program and a strong enrichment program. Parents are very supportive of the wide range of school activities. The Parent Council is very active and often political. The Parent Council chairperson and the principal regularly (and historically) disagree on issues.

The following support programs for mathematics are offered:

- Mathematics drill programs are available in the computer lab.
- "Math Backpacks" are used in the primary grades to support problem solving.
- A Family Math Night is being planned.

The following have been implemented in the school to improve literacy skills:

- Emphasis on literacy in all curriculum areas
- First Steps
- Specific strategies for reading and writing regularly shared by teachers
- School exemplars for writing nearing completion in all grades
- Open Court used to support early literacy

CASE STUDY

Elementary

Systemwide Tests, 2007–2008

Grade 2 Reading and Mathematics Test

School and District Performance in Comparison to National Percentiles

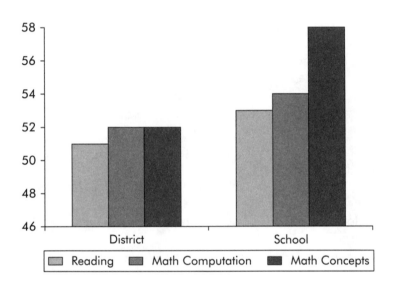

Grade 8 Reading and Mathematics Test

School and District Performance in Comparison to National Percentiles

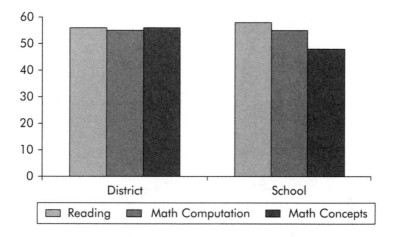

CASE STUDY

Elementary

Student Attitudes in Grade 3 and Grade 6

Reading	Grade 3			Grade 6		
	State	District	School	State	District	School
I like to read.	75%	78%	81%	72%	75%	84%
I am a good reader.	60%	65%	65%	58%	62%	69%
I like to read when I am not in school.	78%	80%	81%	67%	68%	77%

Writing	Grade 3			Grade 6		
	State	District	School	State	District	School
I like to write.	77%	72%	71%	65%	67%	70%
I am a good writer.	70%	75%	75%	70%	74%	77%
I like to write when I am not in school.	66%	64%	68%	58%	59%	70%

Mathematics	Grade 3			Grade 6		
	State	District	School	State	District	School
I like mathematics.	83%	85%	85%	79%	83%	67%
I am a good at mathematics.	70%	74%	75%	66%	67%	55%
I like to do math when I am not in school.	56%	59%	60%	51%	52%	35%

CASE STUDY

Elementary

State Testing: Overall Performance, Grade 3

Percentage of students at Satisfactory level or higher

Reading

Re = Reasoning, Com = Communication, Or = Organization, Ap = Application

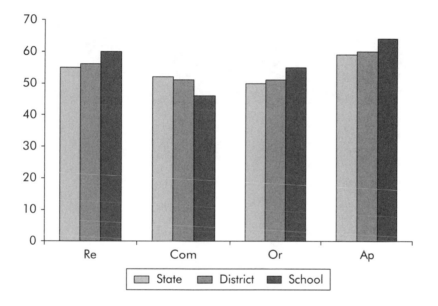

(Continued)

(Continued)

Writing

Re = Reasoning, Com = Communication, Or = Organization,
Ap = Application

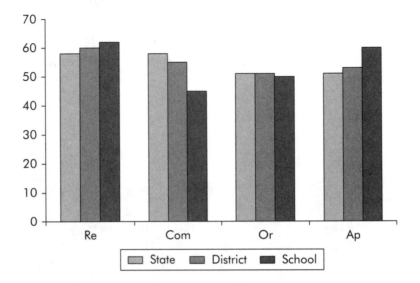

Mathematics

PS = Problem Solving, Co = Concepts, Ap = Application,
Com = Communication

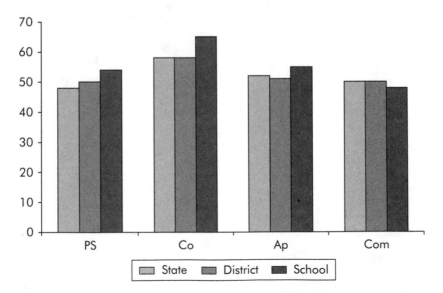

CASE STUDY

Elementary

State Testing: Overall Performance, Grade 6

Percentage of students at Satisfactory level or higher

Reading

Re = Reasoning, Com = Communication, Or = Organization,
Ap = Application

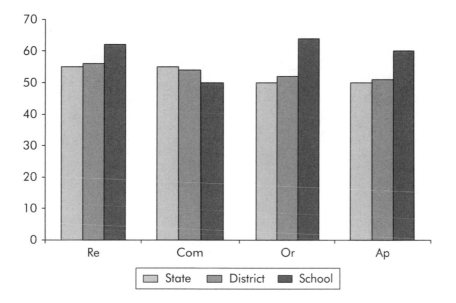

(Continued)

(Continued)

Writing

Re = Reasoning, Com = Communication, Or = Organization, Ap = Application

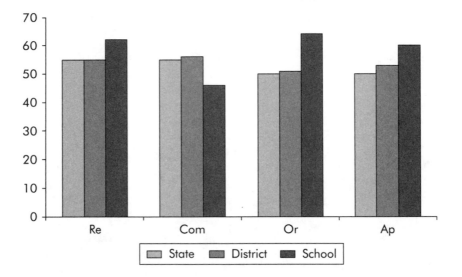

Mathematics

PS = Problem Solving, Co = Concepts, Ap = Application, Com = Communication

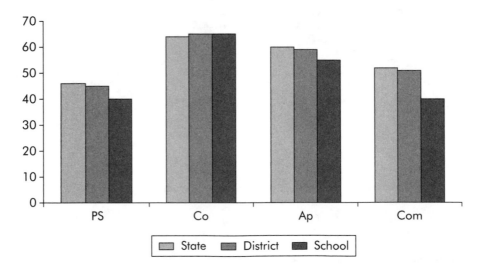

CASE STUDY

Elementary

Satisfaction Surveys

The district administered a satisfaction survey. All ratings were on a five-point scale (Very Satisfied, Satisfied, Undecided, Dissatisfied, Strongly Dissatisfied). The volume of response was sufficient to consider the results valid.

Percentage of Parents Satisfied With the Reading Program

Percentage Very Satisfied/Satisfied

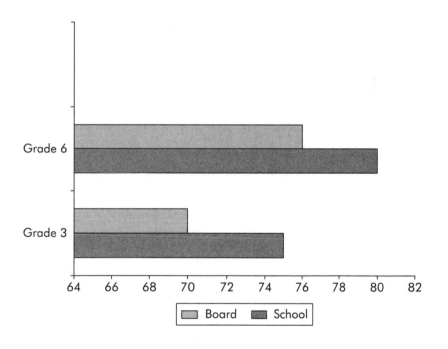

(Continued)

(Continued)

Percentage of Parents Satisfied With the Writing Program

Percentage Very Satisfied/Satisfied

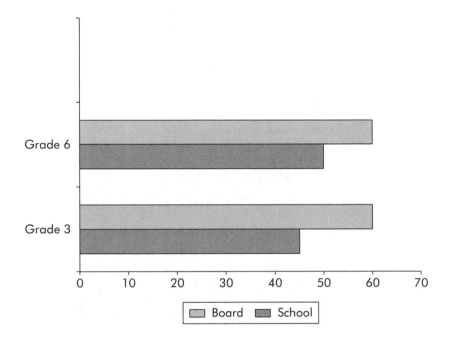

Percentage of Parents Satisfied With the Mathematics Program

Percentage Very Satisfied/Satisfied

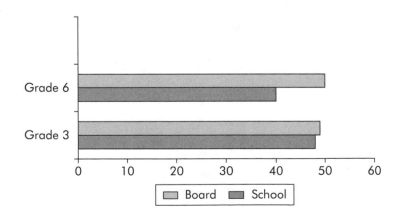

Resource D: Case Study—Secondary

School Demographics:

Enrollment by grade:

Grade 9   442

Grade 10   425

Grade 11   401

Grade 12   295

Total   1,563

Location: Large urban center

Number of languages represented in the school: 53

% of students and/or parents who have immigrated to country: 87

% of students with primary language other than English: 69

% of students new to the school between September and June: 28

Number of years in country:

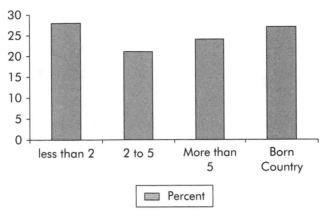

62 students (4% of population) are deemed exceptional (learning disabilities).

Curriculum

Most of the students in this school intend to continue their education at college or university. About 10 percent of the course enrollments in Grade 9 are at the lower level, for non-college-bound students.

In addition to emphasizing high academic achievement, school staff emphasizes community service and participation in athletics, cultural activities, and other extracurricular events and programs.

The following support programs for mathematics are offered:

- Teacher and peer tutors during lunchtime and after school
- Math labs with computers
- Extra assistance through a resource center for at-risk students

The following have been implemented in the school to improve literacy skills:

- A peer tutor program
- First Steps
- Emphasis on literacy in all curriculum areas
- Specific strategies for reading and writing
- Instruction about conducting independent research

CASE STUDY

Secondary

Credit Accumulation for 16-Year-Olds

The completion of 16 credits by the time the student is 16 is a predictor of successful school completion. This represents the completion of a full program in Grades 9 and 10. A number of factors may contribute to students' completing a full program. One is the stability and continuity of a student's program in a school. For this reason, credit information is reported for the two groups of students listed below:

- Students who have been in the district for their full program for Grades 9 and 10 (250 students in this school)
  - 70 percent of this group of 16-year-olds in this school attained 16 or more credits. (This was 73 percent for the district as a whole.)
  - 15 percent attained 15.5 or 15 credits.
  - 4 percent attained 14.5 or 14 credits.
- Students who arrived in the district after the beginning of their Grade 9 program (175 students in this school)
  - 62 percent of this group of 16-year-olds in this school attained 16 or more credits. (This was 53 percent for the district.)
  - 14 percent attained 15.5 or 15 credits.
  - 2 percent attained 14.5 or 14 credits.

Dropout Rate

3 percent of students left this school during the school year but did not graduate or register in another school. The district rate is 5 percent.

Graduation Rate

71 percent of the students who started in this school in Grade 9 graduated by the time they were 19 years old.

(Continued)

(Continued)

Suspension Data

Year	# of Suspensions	As % of Pop.
2005–2006	48	3.07%
2006–2007	70	4.48%
2007–2008	74	4.73%

CASE STUDY

Secondary

Absenteeism and Average Marks

Course	Average # of days absent (semester)		Average course mark	
	School	District	School	District
Grade 9				
Math (Academic)	6	6	62	66
English (Academic)	12	4	69	62
Science (Academic)	5	8	73	74
Geography (Academic)	5	7	69	68
Music (Open)	4	3	73	72
Drama(Open)	5	4	73	74
Grade 11				
Math (University/College)	8	9	70	72
English (University/College)	15	6	73	71
Science (University/College)	7	8	72	75
Geog. (University/College)	10	8	71	69
Music (All Courses)	5	4	74	73
Drama (All Courses)	5	4	74	71
Grade 12				
Math Functions & Calculus	9	7	61	64
Math Data Management	10	9	59	61
Math Geometry & Discrete	7	7	66	70
Math Algebra (College)	12	14	74	70
English (University)	13	10	72	74
English (College)	14	12	68	72
Chemistry	7	8	74	75
Physics	6	8	69	68
Biology	11	7	71	72
World Issues	9	10	74	71

CASE STUDY

Secondary

Achievement Test Results for Grade 9

Grade 9 students wrote the literacy sections of a nationally normed achievement test in the fall and in the spring. Level 18 was administered in the fall, and Level 19 was administered in the spring. The results below show how students in this school ranked in literacy compared to other students in the same grade at the same time of year.

Percentile Rank Corresponding to Average Scores

LE = Language Expression, Sp = Spelling, RC = Reading Comprehension

S = School, D = District

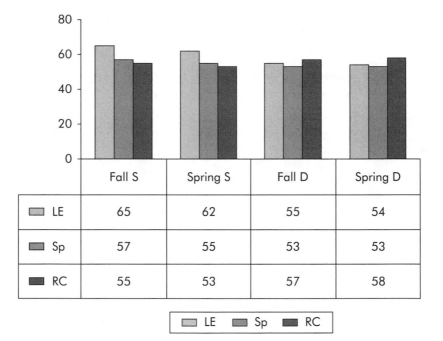

	Fall S	Spring S	Fall D	Spring D
▨ LE	65	62	55	54
▨ Sp	57	55	53	53
▨ RC	55	53	57	58

LE   Sp   RC

Grade 9 Writing

Students in Grade 9 also wrote an expository composition about a history topic. This composition was rated on a four-point holistic scale, using anchors developed by the district. Level 3 (of 4) matched the curriculum standard developed by the state. The district established a target of 75 percent of students achieving level 3.

Percent of students at levels 3 or 4 in Grade 9 writing assignment:

Year	School	District
2006–2007	61%	68%
2007–2008	63%	75%

CASE STUDY

Secondary

Grade 12 Mathematics (University/College)

The district has a common final exam for all students in each Grade 12 university mathematics course.

The overall results for the last three years:

	2005–2006		2006–2007		2007–2008	
	Avg.	Students	Avg.	Students	Avg.	Students
School	55%	178	58%	193	62%	180
District	58%	3,258	60%	3,296	68%	3,281

School results for Grade 12 mathematics by course (or equivalent course 2005–2008):

Course	2005–2006	2006–2007	2007–2008
Functions & Calculus	54%	57%	61%
Data Management	61%	56%	59%
Geometry & Discrete	50%	60%	66%
Total test	55%	58%	62%

CASE STUDY

Secondary

Satisfaction Surveys

The district administered a satisfaction survey. All ratings were on a five-point scale. The volume of response was sufficient to consider the results valid.

How satisfied are you that the school is a safe place in which to learn?

Percentage Very Satisfied/Satisfied

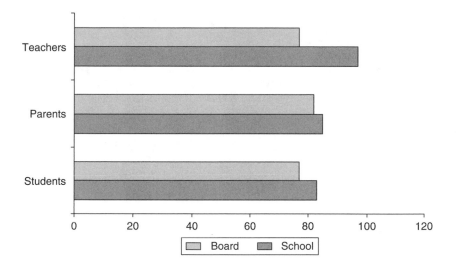

(Continued)

(Continued)

To what extent are students encouraged to set high expectations in school courses?

Percentage Always/Usually

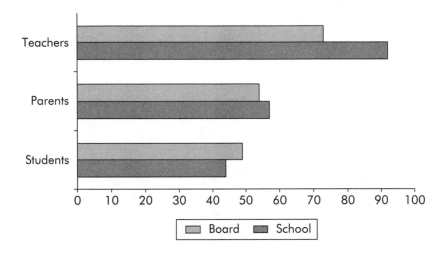

How satisfied are you with achievement in English?

Percentage Very Satisfied/Satisfied

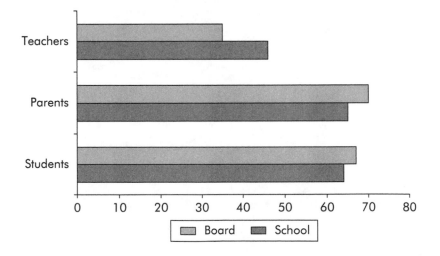

How satisfied are you with achievement in mathematics?

Percentage Very Satisfied/Satisfied

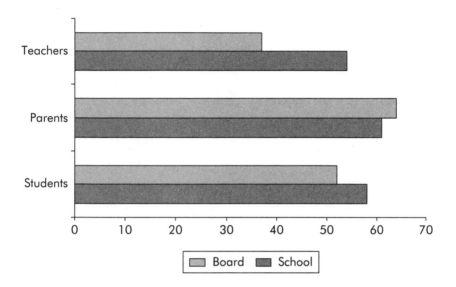

Resource E: Brainstorming
Organization Chart Template 1

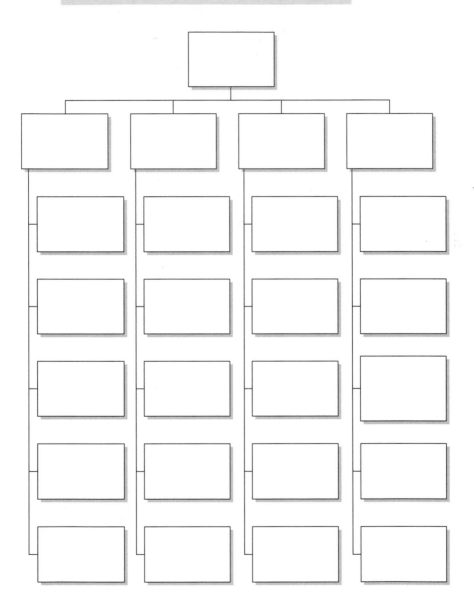

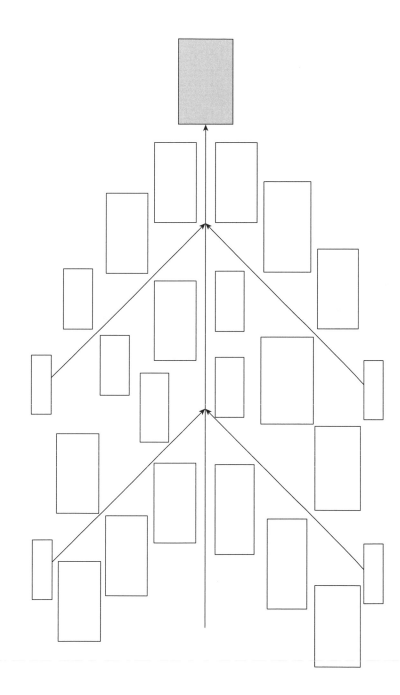

Suggested Additional Readings

Books

Barlosky, M., & Lawton, S. (1994). *Developing quality schools: A handbook.* Toronto, Canada: Ontario Institute for Studies in Education. (ERIC Document Reproduction Service No. ED437705)

Bernhardt, V. L. (2003). *Using data to improve student learning in elementary schools.* Larchmont, NY: Eye on Education.

Bernhardt, V. L. (2004). *Data analysis for continuous school improvement* (2nd ed.). Larchmont, NY: Eye on Education.

Bernhardt, V. L. (2005a). *Using data to improve student learning in high schools.* Larchmont, NY: Eye on Education.

Bernhardt, V. L. (2005b). *Using data to improve student learning in middle schools.* Larchmont, NY: Eye on Education.

Bernhardt, V. L. (2006). *Using data to improve student learning in school districts.* Larchmont, NY: Eye on Education.

Bernhardt, V. L. (2007). *Translating data into information to improve teaching and learning.* Larchmont, NY: Eye on Education

Bostingl, J. J. (2001). *Schools of quality* (3rd ed.). Thousand Oaks, CA: Corwin Press.

Brainard, E. A. (1996). *A hands-on guide to school program evaluation.* Bloomington, IN: Phi Delta Kappa.

Education Quality and Accountability Office (EQAO). (2000). *Educator handbook* (2nd ed.). Toronto, ON, Canada: Queen's Printer for Ontario.

English, F. W. (1999). *Successful schools: Guidebooks to effective educational leadership: Vol 4. Deciding what to teach and test: Developing, aligning, and auditing the curriculum* (Millenium ed.; F. W. English, Series Ed.). Thousand Oaks, CA: Corwin Press.

English, F. W., Frase, L. E., & Arhar, J. M. (1992). *Successful schools: Guidebooks to effective educational leadership: Vol 9. Leading into the 21st century* (F. W. English, Series Ed.). Newbury Park, CA: Corwin Press.

Gallagher, K. S. (1992). *Successful schools: Guidebooks to effective educational leadership: Vol 2. Shaping school policy: A guide to choices, politics, and community relations* (F. W. English, Series Ed.). Newbury Park, CA: Corwin Press.

Herman, J. L., & Winters, L. (1992). *Tracking your school's success: A guide to sensible evaluation.* Newbury Park, CA: Corwin Press.

Holcomb, E. L. (2004). *Getting excited about data: Combining people, passion, and proof to maximize student achievement* (2nd ed.). Thousand Oaks, CA: Corwin Press.

Kaufman, R. (1994). *Successful schools: Guidebooks to effective educational leadership: Vol 1. Mapping educational success: Strategic thinking and planning for school administrators* (rev. ed.; F. W. English, Series Ed.). Thousand Oaks, CA: Corwin Press.

Leithwood, K., Aitken, R., & Jantzi, D. (2006). *Making schools smarter: Leading with evidence* (3rd ed.). Thousand Oaks, CA: Corwin Press.

Lezotte, L. W., & Jacoby, B. C. (1990). *A guide to the school improvement process based on effective schools research.* Okemos, MI: Effective Schools Products and Michigan Institute for Education Management.

Lipton, L., & Wellman, B. (2004). *Data-driven dialogue: A facilitator's guide to collaborative inquiry.* Sherman, CT: MiraVia.

Murgatroyd, S., & Morgan, C. (1992). *Total quality management and the school.* Buckingham, England: Open University Press.

O'Neill, J., & Conzemius, A. (with Commodore, C., & Pulsfus, C.). (2006). *The power of SMART goals: Using goals to improve student learning.* Bloomington, IN: Solution Tree.

Poston, W. K., Jr., Stone, M. P., & Muther, C. T. (1992). *Successful schools: Guidebooks to effective educational leadership: Vol 7. Making schools work: Practical management of support operations* (F. W. English, Series Ed.). Newbury Park, CA: Corwin Press.

Sagor, R., & Barnett, B. G. (1994). *The TQE principal: A transformed leader.* Thousand Oaks, CA: Corwin Press.

Schmoker, M. J. (1999). *RESULTS: The key to continuous school improvement* (2nd ed.). Alexandria, VA: Association for Supervision and Curriculum Development.

Schmoker, M. J., & Wilson, R. B. (1993). *Total quality education: Profiles of schools that demonstrate the power of Deming's management principles.* Bloomington, IN: Phi Delta Kappa.

Stoll, L., & Fink, D. (1996). *Changing our schools: Linking school effectiveness and school improvement.* Buckingham, UK: Open University Press.

Sutton, R. (1994). *Managing school self-review: A practical approach.* Salford, England: Author.

Willms, J. D. (2002). *Monitoring school performance: A guide for educators.* Washington, DC: RoutledgeFalmer.

Woodward, C. A., & Chambers, L.W. (1980). *Guide to questionnaire construction and question writing.* Ottawa, ON: Canadian Public Health Association.

Articles/Papers

Smith, W. J., Moos, L., & MacBeath, J. (1998, April). *School self-assessment: Quality in the eye of the stakeholder.* Draft version of paper presented at the annual meeting of the American Educational Research Association (AERA), San Diego, CA.

Stoll, L. (1992). *Perceptions of implementation of the school growth planning process in Halton Schools.* Burlington, Ontario: Halton Board of Education.

Internet Resources

Association for Effective Schools (http://www.mes.org): The Association for Effective Schools strives "to fulfill its mission by delivering professional development activities (to teachers, administrators and others); providing supportive products, resources and services; and recognizing school success."

National Quality Institute (NQI; http://www.nqi.ca): Mission is to help "organizations to continuously improve performance and results by providing innovative national criteria, progressive implementation programs, services and certification." Offers a variety of assessment tools.

Office for Standards in Education, Children's Services and Skills (Ofsted; http://www.ofsted.gov.uk): Ofsted "inspect[s] and regulate[s] to achieve excellence in the care of children and young people, and in education and skills for learners of all ages." Web site includes publications and research section.

Glossary

Accountability: A process by which educators are held responsible for performance outcomes.

Assessment: The practice of collecting information about what learners know and can do. Includes both qualitative and quantitative data used to make judgments about what students know and should learn next.

Benchmark: A standard against which performance can be judged. Benchmarks can be used to monitor the rate of progress toward meeting goals.

Criterion-referenced test: A test that measures an individual's performance against a well-specified set of standards (as opposed to a norm-referenced test).

Data warehouse: A central repository, usually electronic, for data collected by a system. It is usually a collection of (sometimes linked) databases.

Demographic data: Information including race, gender, socioeconomic status, first languages, and other descriptive data.

Disaggregation: Breaking down data into its constituent groups (e.g., by age, socioeconomic status, or gender).

Evaluation: The process of assigning meaning to the data collected on learners. Evaluation may focus on either what the learner can do or what the learner cannot do.

Formative assessment: Assessment during the learning phase with the primary intention of guiding the instructional process.

Longitudinal data: Information collected consistently over years to track growth, progress, and change.

Mean: An arithmetic average—that is, the sum of the values of all the observations divided by the number of observations.

Median: The value above and below which half the data fall. This measure is less influenced than the mean by extreme values.

Mode: The most frequently occurring value(s).

Norm-referenced test: A test that measures an individual's performance against that of a larger group, usually a national sample representing a diverse cross section of students (as opposed to a criterion-referenced test).

Outcome data: Information about the performance of individuals or groups.

Perceptual data: Information about what individuals or groups think about a particular object, process, or outcome.

Process data: Information about how things are done.

Qualitative data: Data based on information gathered from interviews, solicited comments, focus groups, or general observations over time.

Quantitative data: Data based on numbers.

Reliability: The degree to which a test consistently measures what it is supposed to measure; the degree to which a test supports a complete and accurate measurement of a student's performance across time and tasks.

Rubric: A set of rules or criteria to give direction to the scoring of a piece of work or work sample.

Scale score: A standard score that permits comparisons from grade to grade across time and among different forms of a test.

Standardized test: A test that is administered, scored, and interpreted exactly the same way each time it is administered.

Stanine scores: A standard score of nine units in which 1, 2, and 3 indicate below average performance; 4, 5, and 6 indicate average performance; and 7, 8, and 9 indicate above average performance.

Summative assessment: An assessment at the end of a period of learning that is designed to demonstrate how well a student has learned the knowledge and/or skills taught.

Triangulation: Combining three or more sources (or investigators or methods, etc.) of data to get a more complete and valid picture.

Validity: The degree to which a test measures what it is actually supposed to measure.

References

American Association of School Administrators (AASA). (2002). *Using data to improve schools: What's working.* Arlington, VA: Author. Retrieved August 10, 2008, from http://www.aasa.org/files/PDFs/Publications/UsingDataToImproveSchools.pdf

Bernhardt, V. L. (1998). *Data analysis for comprehensive school improvement.* Larchmont, NY: Eye on Education.

Brown, J., & Isaacs, D. (1996/1997). Conversation as a core business process. *The Systems Thinker 7*(10). Retrieved August 10, 2008, from http://www.theworldcafe.com/articles/CCCBP.pdf

Conference Board of Canada. (2000). *Employability skills 2000+.* Ottawa, ON, Canada: Author. Retrieved August 11, 2008, from http://www.conferenceboard.ca/education/learning-tools/employability-skills.htm

Conzemius, A., & O'Neill, J. (2002). *The handbook for SMART school teams.* Bloomington IN: National Educational Service.

Covey, S. (2001). *The 4 roles of leadership.* (Workshop handbook available from the Premier imprint of FranklinCovey, 2200 West Parkway Blvd., Salt Lake City, UT 84119; 800-827-1776; http://www.franklincovey.com)

Earl, L. M., & Katz, S. (2006). *Leading schools in a data-rich world: Harnessing data for school improvement.* Thousand Oaks: Corwin Press.

Education Improvement Commission, Ontario Ministry of Education. (2000). *School improvement planning: A handbook for principals, teachers, and school councils.* Toronto, ON, Canada: Author.

Greenblatt, A. (2007, September). Teaching past the test: Schools are leveraging data collected for No Child Left Behind to improve individual student performance. *Governing, 20*(12), p. 26+. Retrieved August 10, 2008, from http://www.governing.com/articles/9nclb.htm

Lezotte, L. W. (1991). *Correlates of effective schools: The first and second generation.* Okemos, MI: Effective School Products.

National Reading Panel. (2000). *Teaching children to read: An evidence-based assessment of the scientific research literature on reading and its implications*

for reading instruction. Retrieved August 10, 2008, from http://www
.nationalreadingpanel.org/Publications/publications.htm

Ontario Ministry of Education. (2008). *Boys' literacy.* Retrieved August
10, 2008, from http://www.edu.gov.on.ca/eng/curriculum/boys
literacy.html

Partnership for 21st Century Skills. (2007). *Framework for 21st century
learning.* Tucson, AZ: Author. Retrieved August 10, 2008, from
http://www.21stcenturyskills.org/documents/frameworkflyer_
072307.pdf

Preuss, P. G. (2003). *A school leader's guide to root cause analysis: Using
data to dissolve problems.* Larchmont, NY: Eye on Education.

State of Washington, Superintendent of Public Instruction. (2006).
School improvement. Retrieved August 11, 2008, from http://www
.k12.wa.us/schoolImprovement/default.aspx

Technology Alliance. (2005). *Paradigm shift to data-driven decision making.*
Retrieved August 10, 2008, from http://www.technology-alliance
.com/pubspols/dddm/paradigmshift.html

U.S. Department of Education. (2008). *Foundations of success: The final report
of the National Mathematics Advisory Panel.* Retrieved August 10, 2008,
from http://www.ed.gov/about/bdscomm/list/mathpanel/index.html

Index

CORWIN PRESS

The Corwin Press logo—a raven striding across an open book—represents the union of courage and learning. Corwin Press is committed to improving education for all learners by publishing books and other professional development resources for those serving the field of PreK–12 education. By providing practical, hands-on materials, Corwin Press continues to carry out the promise of its motto: **"Helping Educators Do Their Work Better."**

ONTARIO
PRINCIPALS'
COUNCIL

The Ontario Principals' Council (OPC) is a voluntary professional association for principals and vice-principals in Ontario's public school system. We believe that exemplary leadership results in outstanding schools and improved student achievement. To this end, we foster quality leadership through world-class professional services and supports. As an ISO 9001 registered organization, we are committed to our statement that "quality leadership is our principal product."